# DESIGNED
# TO FAIL

# DESIGNED TO FAIL

*Why Racial Equity in School Funding Is So Hard to Achieve*

## Roseann Liu

The University of Chicago Press

*Chicago and London*

The University of Chicago Press, Chicago 60637
The University of Chicago Press, Ltd., London
© 2024 by The University of Chicago
Published 2024
Printed in the United States of America

33  32  31  30  29  28  27  26  25  24     1  2  3  4  5

ISBN-13: 978-0-226-83269-2 (cloth)
ISBN-13: 978-0-226-83271-5 (paper)
ISBN-13: 978-0-226-83270-8 (e-book)
DOI: https://doi.org/10.7208/chicago/9780226832708.001.0001

Library of Congress Cataloging-in-Publication Data
Names: Liu, Roseann, author.
Title: Designed to fail : why racial equity in school funding is so hard to achieve /
   Roseann Liu.
Description: Chicago : The University of Chicago, 2024. | Includes bibliographical
   references and index.
Identifiers: LCCN 2023035267 | ISBN 9780226832692 (cloth) | ISBN 9780226832715
   (paperback) | ISBN 9780226832708 (ebook)
Subjects: LCSH: Public schools—United States—Finance. | Discrimination in
   education—United States. | Racial justice in education.
Classification: LCC LB2825 .L595 2024 | DDC 370.80973—dc23/eng/20230807
LC record available at https://lccn.loc.gov/2023035267

♾ This paper meets the requirements of ANSI/NISO Z39.48-1992
(Permanence of Paper).

*For Stan and Rochelle, who get things done.*

# CONTENTS

# A Critical Race Perspective on School Funding

Nationwide, there is a $23 billion school funding gap between majority-white and nonwhite districts (EdBuild 2019). In Pennsylvania, a 2016 study revealed racial bias in the school funding system. The findings demonstrated that the whiter the school district, the more state funding it received relative to its fair share; the more Black and Brown students in a school district, the less state funding it received relative to its fair share, when controlled for poverty and other factors (Mosenkis 2016). These findings come over forty years after civil rights legislation outlawed discrimination based on race. *How then does the racial school funding gap[1] persist today despite race-neutral policies?* Relatedly, *why is racial equity in school funding so hard to achieve?*

★ ★ ★

On June 12, 2019, over one thousand people from across the state of Pennsylvania boarded buses and trains headed to Harrisburg to rally for fair school funding. The rally was timed to coincide with budget negotiations and was strategically located in the state capitol building to pressure state legislators to change Pennsylvania's inequitable distribution of education aid. As the ground floor of the capitol rotunda swelled with people, the crowd moved up the grand staircase, creating a cascade of red T-shirts that flowed from the fourth-floor mezzanine. The rally was coordinated by POWER, a faith-based, grassroots organizing group that has made racial equity in school funding a centerpiece of its work. POWER's message was emblazoned on signs that read "END Racial Bias in School Funding," "BLACK MINDS MATTER," and, creatively, "WTF Where's the funding?" Speaking to a reporter who covered the event, a member of POWER animated the way in which disparities in school funding and lack of access to high-quality education are a dimension of the afterlife of slavery (Hartman 2008). Reverend Phyllis Harris, who ministers at an African Methodist Episcopal (AME) church in Philadelphia said: "I believe that this [inequitable funding] is the new form of systematic chains. . . . The new plantation here is education."

A few weeks after this rally, a press event took place in the same location, but with much less fanfare. Flanked by school funding advocates from the PA Schools Work campaign (a coalition of unions and education policy organizations), Governor Wolf and his supporters took credit for the state's $160 million increase in basic education funding (Wolfman-Arent and Mahon 2019), though this was a far cry from the $479 million of additional state education aid that Wolf had proposed (Klehr 2019), and still far less than the $4.6 billion of additional revenue needed to adequately fund schools (Hanna and Fernandez 2020). At the press event, Rich Askey, the president of the Pennsylvania State Education Association (PSEA), the state's teachers' union and one of the lead organizations in PA Schools Work, said he was "proud to stand here today with Gov. Wolf and my fellow education advocates" to acknowledge the "great progress we've made in funding Pennsylvania's public schools."

Republican lawmakers, who have held almost uninterrupted power over the state legislature for eight decades (Rodden 2019:156), were noticeably absent from events such as these. They often fought against increases to the education budget. To Republican leaders, there was nothing wrong with the current school funding system. In fact, proposed increases to the education budget threatened their stance on taxes.

The conflicting perspectives on Pennsylvania's school funding system represented by POWER, PA Schools Work, and Republican legislators provide a window into why change has been so hard to come by. Most Republican leaders in the state legislature represent majority-white districts that benefit from the racial school funding gap. Since they controlled the legislative agenda, policies that would have changed the status quo were never allowed to see the light of day, enabling the persistence of white-district domination—that is, majority-white districts that systematically benefit from the racial gap in school funding. From their vantage point, the school funding system worked just fine, and *if it ain't broke, don't fix it.*

From the viewpoint of the PA Schools Work campaign, additional money for everyone was seen as "great progress," even if it failed to address issues of inequity. Campaign members' relationships with state legislators helped them advance their agenda of increasing the education budget, but these relationships also curtailed what they were willing to ask for. Proposals tended to focus on increasing funding to every school district, rather than bold redistributive solutions aimed at addressing racial disparities.

From POWER's perspective, the racial school funding gap was "the new plantation." While POWER beat the drum of racial inequity in school funding and mobilized everyday citizens through its campaign, legislators consistently turned a colorblind eye to their demands for justice. Within the landscape of Pennsylvania school funding, not all perspectives held equal weight. At the heart of this book is a story of how powerful Republican state leaders and the most politically connected advocates refused to challenge the racial school funding status quo, using their structural power to maintain the advantages accrued to predominantly white districts.

The mindset of Republican leaders—*if it ain't broke, don't fix it*—explains their inclination toward school funding stasis. The system, according to them, worked just fine. In contrast, popular liberal discourses about injustice and inequality often leverage the notion that the system is "broken." This conceptualization presupposes that some *part* of the system is not working properly or fairly for all people. Contrary to both these ideas, this book argues that the problem with the school funding system in Pennsylvania runs much deeper: it was *designed to fail* Black and Brown children. This framing of the problem has significant consequences for *who* we believe should be held accountable, and *what* the necessary next steps are.

In the world of "urban education," *failure* is so often ascribed to Black and Brown children and parents. These culture-of-poverty narratives assert that the failure to adapt to white middle-class values and behaviors is the reason for differential educational outcomes. By arguing that the school funding system is designed to fail our Black and Latine children, this book puts a spotlight on the structures that have failed children and the powerful people who should be held to account for maintaining systems of oppression and inequality. Instead of asking how *students of color* have failed, this book asks how *state legislators and school funding advocates* have failed students of color by actively protecting white districts.

How we understand a problem has consequences for what we believe the necessary next steps are. If we imagine that the problem of school funding is that some part of the system is broken, then our efforts will focus on fixing that part of the system. However, if we think that the problem is a systemwide design failure, then a more systemic approach is required. The racial school funding gap does not exist because we lack technical solutions. Rather, school funding inequity persists because of a structure and culture in the state legislature and in coalitions that protect the school funding privileges of predominantly white districts at a cost to majority-minority school districts. The problem of school funding inequity is far-reaching and systemic, thereby requiring equally far-reaching and systemic redress.

When I argue that the school funding system is designed to fail Black and Brown children, I am not implying that a cabal of state lawmakers gathered in a room to conspire against students of color. While that kind of racial animus is what many people think of when they hear the word *racism*, the kind of racism I document in this book is different from that. In contrast, in more recent years, an understanding of *structural racism* has come into greater public consciousness. "This view characterizes racism as something that lives not in individuals, but in *systems*—in the fabric of American society" (Ewing 2018:12). Eve Ewing analogizes structural racism to a merry-go-round where "the machine is functioning with or without you" (Ewing 2018:13). Racism, in this sense, is "perfectly normal and predictable because [it is] built into the social systems" (Ewing 2018:13).

The kind of racism that this book chronicles does not fit neatly into either of these categories. While there were no instances in which a cabal of people gathered with the expressed intention of underfunding majority-minority districts, it was also not the case that the machinery of racism functioned completely on its own. Rather, the kind of racism that I observed—one that has led to a persistent racial school funding gap in Pennsylvania—is an *agentive* form of structural racism. Extending the metaphor of the merry-go-round, even though racism functions with some automaticity, it still requires the actions of an operator to keep it going. And when it comes to people with the power to make decisions that have widespread impact, their practices should be carefully scrutinized.

The actions of state lawmakers and certain advocates are what kept the political machinery of racist school-funding structures humming. Through a range of policy decisions, they exercised a kind of agency best described as a *willful neglect* for racial equity on the one hand, and an *ever-active stasis* that sought to maintain the existing school funding privileges of majority-white districts on the other. Privileging majority-white districts was a naturalized part of Pennsylvania's political structure and culture, making resistance to equity quite easy and natural. Republican state leaders and some advocates of school funding *knew* the consequences of their policy decisions, but *ignored* the educational harm these decisions would have on students of color, defaulting to the centuries-old norm of protecting and privileging whiteness. Rather than frame the racial school funding gap as a diffused effect of systemic racism that has no clear culprits, I argue that those who occupied positions of political power actively stewarded and were fully invested in maintaining privilege for their majority-white constituents, while practicing a willful neglect toward majority-minority districts.

## RETHINKING "URBAN EDUCATION"

Whenever I teach a course called *Urban Education*, I am tempted to put the title in scare quotes to signal to students that a big part of the course entails deconstructing common deficit-oriented assumptions associated with the term. In her brilliant 1975 talk at Portland State University, Toni Morrison took academia to task for its stunted intellectual pursuits. She contended:

> In 1975 we are left with pretty much the same mental equipment we had in 1775—the equipment that hadn't the curiosity to record the names of human beings in a ship's manifest, hasn't the curiosity

to examine the medieval minds of scientific racists, theologic [*sic*] racists, historical racists, literary racists. (Morrison 1975)

Calling out specific disciplines, she said of urban studies: "Urban studies is the study of Black people, and the approach vigorously held to in these studies: Blacks as wards of the state, never its pioneers" (Morrison 1975). The same critique can be made about urban education.

Classic urban education texts have often been based on what Eve Tuck (2009) refers to as "damage-centered research." Like deficit frameworks that employ transnational culture-of-poverty narratives (Thomas 2009) to explain underachievement, damage-centered research "looks to historical exploitation, domination, and colonization to explain contemporary brokenness, such as poverty, poor health, and low literacy" (Tuck 2009:413). "The danger in damage-centered research," Tuck (2009:41) argues, "is that it is a pathologizing approach in which the oppression singularly defines a community." *Savage Inequalities* (Kozol 1991)—a favorite among undergraduates because of its compelling prose and vivid imagery—comes to mind as an example of a damage-centered urban education text. Though these kinds of texts seek to achieve change by providing a narrative of educational harm, they nevertheless exclusively depict BIPOC (Black, Indigenous, people of color) students as damaged goods.

*Urban education* is commonly associated with racialized pathology and is often used as shorthand for poor or working-class Black and Latine students (Milner 2012), leaving uninterrogated and normalized the notion of *white* and *suburban* (Watson 2012). Though race plays a central role in damage-centered urban education texts, it is often never explicitly analyzed and sometimes not even named. Similar to how colorblindness pervades many academic disciplines, damage-centered urban education texts have "both facilitated and obscured the social reproduction of racial hierarchy" (Crenshaw et al. 2019:1). Because colorblindness serves as the "default intellectual and ethical position for racial justice in many corners of the academy and in public policy" (Crenshaw et al. 2019:4), much of the urban education scholarship has problematically mobilized colorblind portrayals of harm and oppression to seek change.

As an important corrective to colorblind and damage-centered research, more recent urban education texts, many written by Black women scholars, have provided searing analyses of race and racism, moving away from a representation of BIPOCs as singularly defined by oppression. In *Progressive Dystopia*, Savannah Shange (2019) takes the notion of "willful defiance"—language used in the California State Board of Education's disciplinary code that serves as a node in the school-to-prison nexus (Meiners 2007)—and reconceptualizes it as an agentive mode of survivance (Vizenor 2008). As a practice of Black refusal, willful defiance calls into question the legitimacy of the liberal project of statehood and its progressive cognates, asserting that there is no pot of gold at the end of the progressive rainbow.

As well, historical and ethnographic renderings of educational activism in Chicago dispute the image of Black people as only "wards of the state, never its pioneers" (Morrison 1975). Eve Ewing (2018) and Elizabeth Todd-Breland (2018) make visible the labor of Black teachers, parents, students, and community members (oftentimes women), in organizing against top-down reforms that peddle various brands of *bare life* (Agamben 1998) education. *Ghosts in the Schoolyard* (Ewing 2018) shows how Black Chicagoans who protested school closures had a racio-political economic analysis that understood that the policy of school closure was a close cousin to housing policies that displaced the same community less than two decades earlier. In *A Political Education*, Todd-Breland (2018) illustrates how an array of 1960s Black education reformers put forth various Black self-determinist strategies based upon principles of empowerment and self-governance. Instead of portraying Black educators, parents, and students as mere victims, these urban education texts demonstrate the sophisticated analyses and organizing tactics of Black Chicagoans as they sought to change oppressive educational conditions.

Recent books that focus on Philadelphia have also explicitly analyzed the racial politics of urban education and challenged popular notions of victimization. In *Not Paved for Us*, Camika Royal (2022) gives an account of how Constance Clayton, the city's first African American and first woman superintendent (who was much beloved and the longest-tenured superintendent in recent history), refused to play by the colorblind rules that governed the politics of urban education and dared to redistribute resources to schools with the greatest need, which were majority-Black. As a companion piece to *Ghosts in the Schoolyard*, Julia McWilliams's (2019) *Compete or Close* examines the response to school closures and argues that in a precarious urban educational milieu, school leaders sought to stave off closure by racially rebranding their school to create a distinct and unique market niche. By showing how the racial branding of a school as "Asian" pushed out Black students, McWilliams brings a comparative racialization lens to the dynamics of urban education. Royal and McWilliams contribute to our knowledge of how racism operates within a changing market-based system of urban education, and of how people contest conditions not of their making.

In all these texts, which take political economy seriously, the issue of school funding is given treatment as a precipitating factor for the challenges that urban schools face. These authors recognize that disparities in local wealth and the state's insufficient funding have created untenable learning environments for city schools serving students of color. These scholars allude to or make linkages between racist policies and the financial precarity of majority-minority urban school districts. Yet given the analytic focus of these books on other important topics, the connections between racism and school funding are only emergent.

*Designed to Fail* provides a more focused linkage between race and urban school funding, training an analytic eye on how colorblind policies, political structures, and the practices of people in power perpetuate wide and deepening racial disparities in education funding. Invoking Morrison's (1975) critique—that academia "hasn't the curiosity to examine the medieval minds of scientific racists, theologic racists, historical racists, [and] literary racists"—scholars are tasked with "studying up" (Nader 1972) and studying sideways, by applying an analytic lens on the production of racist knowledge, not only in the academy, but also in education policy settings. This book aims to shed light on a central problem in urban education—how and why majority-minority districts are persistently underfunded—by closely examining the protection of white districts by policy actors, and the role of community organizers in contesting that default position.

## ANALYZING SCHOOL FUNDING THROUGH THE LENS
## OF CRITICAL RACE THEORY

If this subset of urban education literature brought race to the foreground as an analytic frame, but positioned school funding in the background, then much of the school funding literature has had the opposite challenge: providing important technical understandings of school funding yet lacking a racial analysis of education finance. In large part, this is because scholarly debates have been consumed by the question of whether money matters when it comes to improving student outcomes. As one researcher recently reflected: "The 'Does money matter?' debate has been getting boring. The idea that increasing school spending wouldn't make the schools work at least a little better probably never made much sense to begin with" (Tyner 2021). And yet because conservative policymakers have consistently cast doubt on proposals to increase education spending by derisively referring to it as "throwing money at a problem," proving that money *does*, in fact, matter was a necessary strand of research.

But today, the debate over the effects of school funding on achievement and other outcomes has largely been settled: money matters when it comes to improving student outcomes (Baker 2016; Jackson 2018; Jackson, Johnson, and Persico 2016; Jackson and Mackevicius 2021; Jackson, Wigger, and Xiong 2021). The two sides largely agree that "we should be striving to improve our education and willing to pay the necessary costs" (Hanushek and Lindseth 2009). As Kirabo Jackson, one of the leading scholars in this area stated, "Researchers should now focus on understanding what kinds of spending increases matter the most" (Barnum 2018). Within the strand of research that focuses on the kinds of education spending that matter, or as an edited volume aptly put it, *Getting the Most Bang for the Education Buck* (Hess and Wright 2020), scholars have shown how teacher-student ratios, teacher salaries, and better-educated teachers affect years of educational attainment (Card and Krueger 1992), and have put forth performance-based models for school spending (Hanushek and Lindseth 2009).

Because money matters, research has also focused on how to get more of it. Equity-minded reports show disparities in school funding by race and economic factors to convey the extent of the problem (e.g.,

Baker, Farrie, and Sciarra 2018; EdBuild 2019; Morgan and Amerikaner 2018; Mosenkis 2016). "Costing out" studies place a dollar amount on how much it costs to provide students a basic education to pressure state legislatures to pony up enough money to reach adequacy (e.g., Augenblick, Palaich and Associates, Inc. 2007). Education law scholars have written about the best strategies for winning school finance lawsuits, especially debating the efficacy of equity- versus adequacy-based arguments, to increase the likelihood of court-mandated school finance reform (e.g., Rebell 2009). In sum, much of the existing literature on school funding has shown that money matters, how it matters, and how to get more of it. But given the evidence that race plays a major role in the distribution of school funding (EdBuild 2019; Kelly 2022; Morgan and Amerikaner 2018; Mosenkis 2016; Public Citizens for Children and Youth 2021) and in the outcome of school finance litigation (Ryan 1999), an equally pressing question to ask is: *How* do race and racism play a role in school funding? Concomitantly, *why* is it so difficult to close the racial school funding gap?

To answer those questions, I turned to critical race theory as a framework for understanding how school funding is disbursed in ways that align remarkably with US and global racial hierarchies (Clarke and Thomas 2006). Instead of viewing racism as an individual or interpersonal problem, critical race theorists have shown how racism is so deeply embedded in laws, policies, and institutions that these systems reproduce white supremacy and racial hierarchy. This perspective brings into relief the policies, structures, and ideologies that uphold the racial school funding status quo. I highlight three concepts that emerged out of the critical race theory literature that have been particularly relevant to this study: interest-convergence, colorblindness, and whiteness as property. Drawing from the research in this book and key writings of critical race scholars, I offer *agentive structural racism* as a fourth piece in the critical race framework. I use the case of *Brown v. Board of Education* as a paradigmatic example that animates these concepts.

## Interest-Convergence

In the decades following landmark civil rights cases like *Brown v. Board of Education* (1954), critical race scholars reflected on why these legal victories produced so little change. Derrick Bell, who as a young lawyer had crafted some of the legal strategies used by the NAACP in *Brown*, looked back at the landmark decision and offered a steely assessment—one that applies to the case of school funding in Pennsylvania today. Bell (2005) did not view the 9–0 unanimous decision to desegregate schools as a watershed moment in the struggle for racial equity in education. Rather, he viewed it as a brief and fleeting moment in which the geopolitical interests of the United States intersected with the interests of Black people. Drawing on Mary Dudziak's (2004) engaging work, Bell believed that the Supreme Court ruled in favor of school desegregation because it bolstered the United States' position in the Cold War by appearing to practice what it preached—that is, values of democracy and equality. Bell referred to the *Brown* ruling as an example of *interest-convergence*—the notion that "the interests of blacks in achieving racial equality will be accommodated only when it converges with the interests of whites" (Bell 1980:523).

The ruling in *Brown II* was seen as evidence of how, when interest-convergence ended, the courts quickly reverted back to decisions that solely supported "the superior social status of whites" (Bell 2005:1059). Traditionally, the courts treated the violation of constitutional rights as grounds for providing *immediate* remedy. And yet in *Brown II*, the court diverged from this well-established tradition. Instead, the justices relinquished authority over local school districts—districts that had been highly resistant to desegregation—and gave them the responsibility to desegregate "with all deliberate speed." Cheryl Harris (1993) and Bell (2005) have noted how the vague and archaic language worked in favor of resistant school districts, allowing them to evade desegregation. "In the foreground was the change of formal societal rules; in the background was the 'natural' fact of white privilege that dictated the pace and course of any moderating change" (Harris 1993:1757).

Interest-convergence also explains the "one step forward, two steps back" pace of change in Pennsylvania school funding. For decades, the state had been criticized for its inadequate and inequitable school funding system. But finally, in 2016, the state legislature adopted what has been colloquially known as the "fair funding formula"—a racially equitable method of distributing school funding—mainly because the interests of Republican state legislators momentarily converged with the interests of majority-minority school districts. Republican governor, Tom Corbett, left office in 2015, suffering a brutal defeat after becoming the poster child of education funding cuts across the state. Faced with a similar prospect of losing elections because of the dismal state of school funding, Republican lawmakers relented and passed legislation in 2016 that established a fair funding formula.

Yet, substantively speaking, this momentary interest-convergence did not do much for majority-minority districts. Though they adopted the fair funding formula, lawmakers also made a policy decision that bolstered racial inequities. Like *Brown II*, state lawmakers were able to defang the effects of the fair funding formula by tinkering with the language of the policy. Although the 2016 law adopted an equitable formula, lawmakers only applied the formula to *new* money—that is, increases to the state education budget. As many observers have noted, an equitable formula is only as good as the money you send through it. Since new money only accounted for about 10 percent of the total state education budget, only 10 percent of state education aid was distributed in a racially equitable manner.

The lion's share of state education funding was distributed through the racially biased policy of *hold harmless*. This policy guarantees that school districts receive at least as much as their allocation in a previous baseline year, regardless of changes in number of students, or the needs of the students. The racial effects of "hold harmless" are clear: white rural districts that have seen a decline in student population are allocated funding levels based on when they had greater numbers of students, while funding for majority-minority urban districts have not kept pace with the increase in their student populations. State lawmakers largely nullified the effects of the fair funding formula through creating an asterisk in the law. The formal status of having an equitable formula did little to improve actual conditions for Black and Latine students. Despite the technical fact of a fair funding formula, the "'natural' fact of white privilege" (Harris 1993:1757) prevailed and dictated the pace of change.

Because "hold harmless" is a central policy mechanism for upholding racial inequity in school funding, race-conscious community organizers consider it a confusing and vexing misnomer. It can only be considered "harmless" from the perspectives of white rural districts that benefit from the policy and their state legislators who benefit from maintaining the support of their constituents. Typically, people are more familiar with the term "hold harmless" as it relates to release forms. Hold harmless clauses release a company from liability for an activity that might cause bodily harm, for example skydiving, go-karting, jumping on trampolines, etc. State lawmakers who adamantly protect the hold harmless policy do so with the hope that maintaining it will release them from the political liability that would surely come if they challenged the school funding privileges that white districts have come to know and enjoy. From the perspective of majority-minority school districts, there is nothing harmless about this policy. Racial justice activists have renamed the policy "hold harmful" to draw attention to the significant harm it has inflicted on majority-Black-and-Latine school districts across the state—a discursive move that I adopt here.

## Colorblindness

Critical race theorists have also argued that while Jim Crow laws were stripped from the books, colorblindness was a new method for maintaining old racial hierarchies. "Colorblindness is a form of race subordination in that it denies the historical context of white domination and Black subordination" (Harris 1993:1768). By pretending not to see race, the system did not have to account for the continuing effects of slavery and Jim Crow. There was no longer a discriminatory law to point to as proof that the system favored whites. The *Brown II* decision keenly illustrates this. The Court's decision that allowed districts to desegregate "with all deliberate speed," was a facially race-neutral statement. And yet the ruling ostensibly allowed for the preservation of school segregation, and the colorblind decision ignored how "implicit racism [can exist] in a racially neutral line of reasoning" (Lawrence 1987:342). The challenge to desegregating was not so much a "technical" one, as the Court claimed, but rather it was the resistance of whites who would have to give up their privileged position (Wasserstrom 1976). Colorblindness has proven to be a highly effective method of maintaining white supremacy; as long as laws and policies are facially race neutral, the system is let off the hook.

Like the story of school desegregation, racist policies in school funding have taken on a new colorblind veneer. During Jim Crow, Black schools were funded through double-taxing Black families, and "despite being tax-paying citizens, blacks found state allocations of resources to be far less for their children's education as compared with white children's" (Givens 2021:1). While education policies are now facially race neutral, today's colorblind school funding policies are linked to de jure policies of the past (Baker and Green 2005). Pennsylvania's hold harmful policy maintains racial inequity in school funding by operating under the colorblind logic of protecting districts that have experienced population decline. Similar in effect to the race-neutral language of desegregating "with all deliberate speed," hold harmful is justified through the race-neutral language of protecting districts that have suffered population loss and rely on "a stable level of funding" because they have "fixed costs" and a "limited tax base."[2]

Colorblindness is also evident in advocacy approaches that emphasize "adequacy"—a call for increased funding for *all* districts. Recalling the words of the president of the teachers' union in the opening vignette, overall increases to *all* school districts were seen as "great progress." Similar to the problem with the slogan *All Lives Matter*, this colorblind "all" approach to school funding ignores the historic inequities between predominantly white and majority-minority school districts. Colorblindness was also evident in "equity" proposals that focused mainly on socioeconomic background, while conspicuously sidestepping race. By "den[ying] the historical context of white domination and Black subordination" (Harris 1993:1768), racial hierarchy was reified through a colorblind approach to school funding.

## Whiteness as Property

I draw on Cheryl Harris's (1993) concept of *whiteness as property* to elucidate the dynamic in which legal entitlements protect white privilege. Property is not always tangible but can be intangible, as in the notion of *intellectual property*. Quoting Bentham, Harris (1993:1729) explains that "property is nothing but the basis of expectation . . . [that one can] draw such and such advantage from the thing possessed." She argues that the law "recognized and protected expectations grounded in white privilege" (Harris 1993:1731). Whiteness became a type of property that was protected by the legal system and conferred to its owners a set of *expectations* and *benefits*. It is "the legal legitimation of expectations of power and control that enshrine the status quo as a neutral baseline, while masking the maintenance of white privilege and domination" (Harris 1993:1715).

Majority-white districts in Pennsylvania enjoyed the settled expectation of school funding privileges. The racial school funding gap was the "neutral baseline." White districts being allocated more than their fair funding formula calculation was the norm. The argument that students of color were suffering from hold harmful held little sway with politicians because they understood that taking away the settled expectation of white constituents was political suicide. Nowhere was this more evident than in discussions about eliminating hold harmful, with legislators and advocates frequently referring to that proposition as a "nonstarter." Eliminating hold harmful was a nonstarter because white districts were accustomed to their comparative school funding advantages and expected to hold onto it in the same way that property rights are protected in this country and cannot be infringed upon. The right to white-district privilege was protected by the policy of hold harmful and trumped the right to equal treatment.

### Agentive Structural Racism

As a framework, critical race theory has made important interventions in raising public consciousness around how legal (and other) institutions reflexively reproduce racism. An aspect of critical race scholarship that has been less popularized is the role that people with structural power play in maintaining those systems. Judges and politicians make decisions that have a disproportionate impact on society, with their actions overdetermining the laws and policies that govern everyday people. Returning to the *Brown II* example, although the majority opinion to desegregate "with all deliberate speed" was presented as a decision made by "the Court," the institution of the US Supreme Court is represented by nine people, with the chief justice at its helm. It was Chief Justice Earl Warren who wrote the majority opinion and who decided to include the phrase, "with all deliberate speed," drawing on Justice Felix Frankfurter's usage of the phrase five times prior to the

*Brown II* ruling (Ogletree 2004:11). With the inclusion of those four words, these justices consciously made a decision that "offered a palliative to those opposed to *Brown's* directive" (Ogletree 2004:11) and effectively set back the civil rights struggle for equality.

Elucidating the role that these justices played in reneging on the promises of *Brown I* has been important to understanding structural racism. Similarly, this book's conceptual focus on the *agents* of structural racism is intended to put names and faces to those who occupy positions of power and make decisions that uphold the racial school funding status quo. Even when state legislators and advocates were confronted with incontrovertible evidence that their policy decisions maintained racial disparities in school funding, they willfully neglected that information and consciously made choices that enacted white-district domination. Their staunch defense of hold harmful was the primary way in which white-district domination was operationalized.

I use the term *white-district domination* to signal how legislators and advocates (in some cases) proposed policies and made decisions based on the settled expectation that majority-white school districts were entitled to the unfair school funding privileges they historically enjoyed. Initially, I considered using the term *white-district privilege*. But as Zeus Leonardo argues, "the theme of privilege obscures the subject of domination, or the *agent* of actions" (Leonardo 2004:138, italics added). White privilege is "secured by a process of domination, or those acts, decisions, and policies that white subjects perpetrate on people of color" (Leonardo 2004:137). Since this book seeks to reveal the "acts, decisions, and policies" (Leonardo 2004:137) of the racial school funding status quo, *white-district domination* was a more appropriate term. Drawing on the concepts of interest-convergence, colorblindness, whiteness as property, and agentive structural racism, this ethnography offers insight into how school funding systems continue to privilege whiteness in the absence of explicitly discriminatory laws and policies.

## THE CASE OF PENNSYLVANIA'S STATE EDUCATION FUNDING

Whenever I tell people I'm writing a book about school funding, friends and strangers inevitably bring up the issue of property taxes. Many of them come from professional-class backgrounds and are highly attuned to the relationship between schools and property taxes. They shop for houses in "good districts," and they are willing (and able) to pay higher local taxes for these schools. They understand that inequities in school funding are related to different local taxing capacities, with wealthier localities being able to generate more money than poorer ones.

Indeed, the fact that school funding in this country is so heavily reliant on local revenues is a major part of the problem. In the United States, there are three streams of public school revenue: state aid, local contributions, and federal funding. In 2020–2021, on average, states contributed 46.8 percent; local governments chipped in 44.5 percent; and the federal government made up 8.8 percent of school revenues (National Education Association 2022). Since nearly half the total revenue relies on local taxes, this has created what advocates call "have and have-not districts." Take for example the disparities that exist between the School District of Philadelphia and the Lower Merion School District, which border one another. The local revenue raised for Lower Merion is $26,000 per student compared to Philadelphia's per-student local revenue of $7,000. Although Lower Merion taxes itself at a lower rate (17 mills) than Philadelphia (23 mills), it is able to raise $19,000 more per pupil in local revenue than Philadelphia.

State education aid is intended to create a more level playing field by distributing funding more *equitably*—that is, according to the needs of students. It is widely agreed that more funding should be distributed to school districts with more economically disadvantaged students, more English learners (ELs), and more students with special needs. It is not enough to give students *equal* funds if some students already have major advantages over others. The equity principle is compromised when a state makes a low contribution to the total revenue, forcing school districts to rely more heavily on its local taxing capacities. Although states contribute 48.6 percent on average, this varies from state to state. In 2020–2021, Pennsylvania contributed only 37 percent toward total public school revenues, earning it the ignominious reputation of being ranked forty-fifth in the country because of its meager share of state aid toward education (National Education Association 2022).

Some dispute this statistic, pointing out that Pennsylvania is ranked eighth in the nation when it comes to total funding amounts (National

Education Association 2022). But Pennsylvania is only ranked so high in this regard because wealthy districts with high local taxing capacities are boosting the state average. The overall high funding average conceals the vast disparities that exist between school districts. Pennsylvania is also known for having the *third-worst funding gap* between high- and low-wealth districts (Ushomirsky and Williams 2015), making it one of the most inequitable states in the country when it comes to school funding. These dismal rankings are related—the more dependent school districts are on local taxes, the more inequitable the situation. While the friends and strangers I've talked with are right in that inter-district inequities are related to disparities in local property taxes, the Pennsylvania case shows that *state* leaders and *state* aid also bear much responsibility for these inequities, and therefore warrant closer investigation.

Another common assumption is the notion that economics are a proxy for race. Both experts and nonexperts frequently assume that students of color are not as well funded *because* many reside in poorer districts with lower taxation power.[3] According to them, racial disparity in school funding, if it exists, is a residual or secondary effect of poverty. This assumption is reflected in the many reports and literature on school finance that analyze the relationship between school funding and levels of poverty but fail to directly examine the relationship between *race* and *school funding*.

Pennsylvania's problem of disparities in school funding isn't simply an economic one; it's also a racial one. In 2014 and 2016, David Mosenkis, a data scientist and member of POWER, published the finding that racial bias exists in the distribution of state aid. When comparing Pennsylvania school districts that had similar levels of poverty (i.e., controlling for poverty), whiter school districts received proportionately more state aid than districts with fewer white students for *every level of poverty* (Mosenkis 2014). The largest racial school funding gap existed between districts at the 50–60 percent poverty decile. At that poverty level, districts serving more white students than the median white population received on average $6,241 of state basic education funding per pupil, while districts serving fewer white students than the median received on average $3,634 of state funding per pupil—a difference of $2,607 per student.

The 2016 study estimated that Philadelphia, a majority-minority school district, received $400 million less than its "fair share," or how much it would have received if all state aid were run through the fair funding formula (Mosenkis 2016). By showing that there was a *racial* bias in *state* aid, these findings challenged two prevailing assumptions: that school funding disparities were primarily economic, and that inequities were only the result of local wealth disparities. Though the 2014 and 2016 findings were published as part of POWER's campaign demanding that the state legislature change Pennsylvania's unjust funding conditions, the general finding that Black and Latine students are disproportionately negatively affected by the state's school funding policy have been confirmed by other research (cf. Kelly 2022).

These racial disparities in funding have had consequences on students' access to educational opportunities. Although Pennsylvania ranks above average in students' access to educational opportunities, a report found that "disparities by race/ethnicity and income are stark" (Shaw-Amoah and Lapp 2020:2). Like the statistics for school funding, Pennsylvania's high ranking in access to educational opportunities (fifteenth in the nation) is boosted by white and Asian American students' high access (eleventh and thirteenth in the nation, respectively), obscuring Black and Latine students' lower access to these opportunities (thirtieth and twenty-eighth in the nation, respectively). The report found that while "race and income disparities in access to educational opportunity exist in most states, the size and pervasiveness of PA's gaps are among the most severe in the country" (Shaw-Amoah and Lapp 2020:2). Pennsylvania's racial school funding gap has undoubtedly played a role in creating the racial educational opportunity gap.

## AN ETHNOGRAPHY OF SCHOOL FUNDING

Pennsylvania's school funding problems have catalyzed advocates and organizers to create change and have elicited actions (or deliberate non-actions) from the state legislature. This constellation of activities and events makes Pennsylvania a valuable case for understanding more broadly the political challenges that stand in the way of creating racially equitable school funding systems. Methodologically, much of the scholarship on school funding has examined laws, policies, and court rulings that are finalized and complete. This approach tends to analyze the *effects* of decisions rather than their *formulation*, thereby obfuscating processes like how an agenda is formed, by whom, and its uptake by various actors. Without such knowledge, school funding decisions are depicted as a fait accompli and the obstacles that stand in the way of a racially equitable school funding system remain unclear, leading to superficial recommendations.

For example, increasing state aid is a common recommendation for mitigating inequities, and yet state legislators can use their "tricks of the trade" (Baker and Green 2005) to maintain racial inequities through various means (see also Vaught 2009). This is what happened in Pennsylvania—though state funding was increased, racial disparities grew (Mosenkis 2020). *Designed to Fail* approaches school funding decisions as contingent and unpacks what these tricks of the trade are and the underlying structures that enable or disable these practices. This book provides a historically informed and ethnographically fine-grained understanding of school funding decisions, allowing us to peer into the processes by which decisions get made, to better understand why so much activity produces so little change, and to collectively press for change in a more informed way. The two main sites of study were the Pennsylvania state legislature and Pennsylvania's school funding campaigns, with the bulk of fieldwork occurring between 2018 and 2020.

## Pennsylvania State Legislature

Since state legislatures bear primary responsibility for determining how school districts are funded, they also bear primary responsibility for the racial school funding gap. As such, I examined the Pennsylvania General Assembly to understand the dominant ideologies and structures that protect white-district domination. I focused on the events, people, and documents that animated key school funding policies. Policies are "the manifest intentions of power elites for the distribution of social goods" (Levinson, Sutton, and Winstead 2009:772). Because "authorized policy functions as ideology" (Levinson, Sutton, and Winstead 2009:774), examining a policy reveals the ideologies that guide the distribution of social goods like school funding. To study the ideology of a particular policy is to understand how this "serves to establish and sustain relations of domination" (Thompson 1990:19) like the racial school funding status quo. Since law, politics, and education are spheres of cultural (re)production that reinscribe racial hierarchy (Hall 2002), examining these spheres, specifically in the context of school funding, provides a window into how racial hierarchy is reproduced.

I focused on the policy of hold harmful because it is one of the central ways in which racial disparity in Pennsylvania state education funding is maintained. Despite the creation of the 2016 fair funding formula, the formula was only applied to increases in the state education budget, with the rest of the budget allocated according to hold harmful. Rather than distributing state aid dynamically, according to a district's changing student enrollment and what those students' needs are, hold harmful guarantees that school districts receive at least as much as they received during a baseline year, regardless of increases or decreases to student enrollment. Most of Pennsylvania's education aid to school districts is based on outdated population data from 1991, or three decades ago (McCorry 2016d). While hold harmful benefits white rural districts that have seen declines in their student populations since the 1990s, it comes at a cost to majority-minority urban districts, many of which have experienced growth in student enrollment since the 1990s. The hold harmful policy has been adamantly protected by powerful state legislators.

Similar to how politicians manipulate legislative district boundaries in cases of gerrymandering to ensure political and material advantage, state legislators' insistence on using outdated student enrollment data manipulates school funding in ways that ensure their majority-white districts' advantage. This anti-democratic practice is akin to malapportionment of student enrollment and gives an unfair advantage to white rural districts whose school funding interests are overrepresented proportionate to their numbers. Focusing on the policy of hold harmful brings into view the tricks of the trade of state politicians—how they can exploit mundane student enrollment data in ways that privilege their constituents—as well as how gerrymandering helps politicians maintain their power to exercise these tricks of the trade.

To understand this policy and the tricks of the trade of politicians, I interviewed sixteen Pennsylvania state legislators and two legislative staffers—twelve of whom were Democrats, and six of whom were Republicans. These interviews provided an understanding of the underlying beliefs and values used to justify hold harmful, as well as the structures of the state legislature that allow hold harmful to prevail. Two additional interviews with state legislators from Ohio and Delaware were conducted and served as useful comparative examples.

## Campaigns for Fair Funding

In addition to studying who makes policy, I was also interested in the "agency of local actors who engage with, or resist, policy in different ways" (Levinson, Sutton, and Winstead 2009:769). Within the landscape of school funding, there is a fairly pronounced gendered division of labor—one in which men tend to dominate the spaces of statehouses and courthouses, and women are more heavily represented in advocacy and organizing work. The literature on school funding mirrors this gender divide. More attention is paid to statehouses and courthouses as sites for studying issues of school funding (e.g., Hanushek and Lindseth 2009; Jackson, Johnson, and Persico 2016; Rebell 2009), and far less attention is given to the work of advocates and organizers (for exception, see Paris 2010), even though they do much to shape public opinion, which is an important factor in sustaining school finance reform (Reed 2001). The methodological choice to examine the work of advocates and organizers elucidates an underexamined aspect of the school funding landscape that is oftentimes occupied by women, namely, how people work to create on-the-ground change and influence public perceptions.

I "follow[ed] the conflict" (Marcus 1995:110) and paid close attention to disputes over the meanings of school funding equity. I conducted interviews with fifteen school funding advocates (five from POWER, nine from PA Schools Work, and one from an unaffiliated organization) to trace the story of how the Campaign for Fair Education Funding split into two campaigns (POWER and PA Schools Work) because of a dispute over what "fair" meant, and especially over whether to emphasize race in their understanding of fairness. This book provides a behind-the-scenes look at the heterogeneous approaches to advocating for school funding and reveals how colorblind approaches hinder the work of advancing racial equity.

## Thick Solidarity as Methodology

What most enables me to write this ethnography is not anything mentioned above or any lines that appear on my CV. Rather, it is a commitment to bearing witness and being adjacent to those who are "closest to the pain," as POWER organizers often liked to say. As a graduate of and former teacher in New York City public schools, that pain was not wholly unfamiliar to me. I attended one of the city's magnet high schools, where there was one very frazzled guidance counselor for over twenty-five hundred students. As a teacher, basic resources—paper, manipulatives, books—frequently came out of my own pocket.

And yet, though I attended city public schools and have children in Philly public schools, I've never had an experience in which the school was so starved of resources that there weren't enough books for students, as a Philadelphia parent testified to in Pennsylvania's landmark school funding trial (Education Law Center 2014). I did not experience this parent's anxiety, disappointment, and anger in discovering that her child had not reached math proficiency for the fourth straight year because of lack of support staff. I did not have firsthand experience of my children's school flooding, and the ceiling collapsing after consecutive days of rain, as occurred at a South Philly high school in 2018 (Graham 2018). Lastly, I identify as Asian American, but the students most directly impacted by underfunding are Black and Latine.

To write as an engaged anthropologist, I practice a mode of *thick solidarity* that is "based on a radical belief in the inherent value of each other's lives despite never being able to fully understand or fully share in the experience of those lives" (Liu and Shange 2018:190). It is "a kind of solidarity that mobilizes empathy in ways that do not gloss over difference, but rather pushes into the specificity, irreducibility, and incommensurability of racialized [and otherwise] experiences" (Liu and Shange 2018:190). Though my coauthor and I originally conceptualized thick solidarity as a mode of political activism, Saudia Garcia pointed out the methodological purchase of this concept in a Tweet, stating that thick solidarity "counter[s] the impetus for thick description . . . giving new language to [ways of being] in ethical relation" with those we share space with in "the field."

I have attempted to write a book that is politically aligned with those I worked with by exposing the structural inequalities of school funding, which Charles Hale (2006:98) refers to as "cultural critique." He differentiates "cultural critique" from "activist research." Though both involve political alignment, activist research "allow[s] dialogue with [collaborators] to shape each phase of the process, from conception of the research topic to data collection to verification and dissemination of the results" (Hale 2006:97). To the extent that the demands of writing a book for tenure allowed me to engage with collaborators in each of these phases, I have also attempted to carry out an activist-oriented ethnographic project, politically fraught as the process is. When I encountered competing perspectives between research participants, I assessed the power and positionality of different group members and tended to align with those who have been historically marginalized and are "closest to the pain."

Thick solidarity *as methodology* is also a gesture toward the need to better thematize the ethnographic backstage and the "background negotiations that rarely make it to the printed page" (Liu 2021:2). If the postmodern turn in anthropology meant that questions like, *Is it authentic?* were replaced by questions like, *Did it break your heart?* (Behar 1996), or *Is it sincere?* (Jackson 2010), then thick solidarity's questions, vis-à-vis engaged anthropology, are more prosaic: *Is it useful? Did it create change?* More than writing an "authentic" ethnography, or even a "sincere" ethnography that "breaks your heart," this ethnography aims to be part of an intersubjective feedback loop that *is* useful and *does* create change.

Ethnographers set out to tell a good story. This is sometimes not readily apparent to students in educational studies who come from different epistemological traditions—often ones in which there are discrete methods to achieve reliability, validity, and generalizability. And so, they often ask questions about how "generalizable" this "one case" is. It's noteworthy that they don't ask these questions when analyzing novels or works of art. As a discipline that is considered a "humanistic social science," anthropology occupies an anxious position that seems to invite these questions and challenges. It is, at once, trying to tell a good story and trying to say something more general. One of my former students, a physics major, took a methods course with me and quickly realized she would need to create a different research paradigm from the one she was familiar with. Instead of asking, *Is it generalizable?* she offered that perhaps more appropriate questions were: *Did it resonate? Is it applicable?*

Though I am telling a particular story about Pennsylvania state legislators and advocates, I hope it has resonances beyond the specific people, places, and events that appear in this ethnography. In the United States, there are thirty-four states that have either a hold harmful provision or something conceptually similar (Atherton and Rubado 2014). While few states apply the hold harmful provision to as large a proportion of their education budget as Pennsylvania, this policy is fairly common and warrants further attention (Kelly 2022). It may be a significant policy mechanism by which racial disparities in school funding are maintained. Therefore, the insights gleaned from the Pennsylvania case may have broader applications for school funding systems across the nation.

While identifying specific policies that enable the racial school funding gap is a useful task, new ones may pop up, distracting us in an endless game of policy whack-a-mole. It is worth remembering the words of Robert L. Carter, a leading NAACP attorney, who understood the bigger picture in *Brown v. Board of Education* and said, "the fundamental vice was not legally enforced racial segregation itself; this was a mere by-product, a symptom of the greater and more pernicious disease—White supremacy" (Carter 1980:23). Similarly, the fight is not against the hold harmful policy per se; the fight is against white supremacist structures that are manifested in the racial school funding gap, zero-tolerance policies, and bans on teaching the truth about race in America, among other assaults.

## BOOK OVERVIEW

*Designed to Fail* gives an inside look at the Pennsylvania state legislature and campaigns for fair funding to understand how different notions of "fairness" were deployed, and why discourses of fairness that privilege white districts so often win out. Chapter 2, "Policies and Structures That Protect White-District Domination," takes a deep dive into the history of the Pennsylvania school funding policy of hold harmful in the 1980s and 1990s to understand how it created a competitive, zero-sum dynamic between poor white rural districts and poor majority-minority urban school districts. Within this context of competition and manufactured scarcity, white rural districts enjoyed outsized political representation, and this tilted the school-funding scales in their favor. This chapter discusses how structures of representative democracy are obstacles to racial equity in school funding, including how vote distribution in a winner-takes-all electoral system favors white rural communities and the Republican Party, how state legislators from rural communities wield great power because they are disproportionately represented in senior leadership, and how gerrymandering by Republican state leaders gives them an unfair political advantage.

Chapter 3, "Stopgap Efforts for a Systemic Problem," describes Pennsylvania's shadow system of school funding, and begins with breaking news in 2013 of closed-door school funding deals by state legislators. Also referred to as "earmarked funding," this process circumvents regular channels of budget appropriations and disproportionately benefits school districts that have legislators in positions of senior leadership. As a regular practice, state legislators secured earmarked funding as a stopgap measure for keeping under-resourced school districts afloat but neglected to find long-term solutions to the problem of inequitable funding. If we see racist school-funding structures as a disease, and lack of resources in school districts as symptoms of that disease, then earmarked funding acted as a sloppily applied Band-Aid that poorly treated some of the symptoms but neglected to find a cure. This chapter shows how earmarked funding had a smoke-and-mirrors effect, obfuscating the public's understanding of the problem and their ability to keep state legislators accountable for finding a long-term, structural solution to racial inequity in school funding.

Chapter 4, "Race-Conscious Losses and Colorblind Wins during the Hornbeck and Rendell Eras," tells the history of school funding coalitions in Pennsylvania and lays the groundwork for understanding how today's colorblind approaches are shaped by past colorblind wins and race-conscious losses. In the early 2000s, David Hornbeck, former superintendent of the School District of Philadelphia, vocally criticized the state for its racist school-funding structure. This created an antagonistic relationship between the school district and Harrisburg politicians—one that was highly unproductive to securing resources for Philadelphia and contributed to the eventual state takeover of Philadelphia schools. In contrast, the golden era of school funding, a brief three-year period, from 2008 to 2011, when Ed Rendell was governor, achieved both a fairly distributed school funding formula and a large increase to the education budget without ever talking about race. Knowing this history allows us to understand present-day coalition politics and why colorblind approaches carry such currency.

Chapter 5, "Speaking with One [Colormute] Voice," looks at the coalitional politics within the Campaign for Fair Education Funding (2014–2018) and how, in the name of speaking in one united voice, the campaign compromised on speaking about racial inequities to appeal to Harrisburg politicians who are allergic to talking about race. State lawmakers reflexively protected the policy of hold harmful and were unwilling to upset their constituents. In their minds, their lack of support to reduce the racial school funding gap was not a vote against majority-minority districts; it was just the way representative democracy works. After all, they were elected to protect the interests of their own (majority-white) constituents who would lose out if the school funding structure changed. I show how beneath the colorblind language to describe districts' needs (e.g., "fixed costs" and "limited tax base") was the settled expectation that state legislators protect the funding privileges of white districts. While the campaign deployed colorblind strategies, POWER began to be more forthright about the racial school funding gap and testified to this during a legislative hearing. While the immediate response from the cochair of the BEF Commission seemed to indicate that they would address the "unintended consequences" of not updating funding formulas, he and the commission ultimately decided to preserve hold harmful, providing a clear example of how people with structural power uphold racial inequities one decision at a time.

Chapter 6, "Displacing Racial Equity," tells the story of the dramatic breakup of the Campaign for Fair Education Funding in 2018. At issue was the role of race in school funding advocacy. While some members, most notably POWER, felt that highlighting the racial gap was central to the campaign, others felt that this was too divisive and that it threatened to pit school districts against one another. Instead, they wanted to take a more colorblind approach that advocated for increasing the overall state education budget—a proposal that they thought all districts could get behind because they all benefited. Their advocacy strategies consistently displaced the issue of racial equity in school funding and eventually led to a split in the campaign, with POWER breaking off and the rest of the members being reconstituted into the new PA Schools Work campaign. Far from changing the racial school funding status quo, these colorblind advocacy strategies reinforced structures of white-district domination.

The final chapter provides an update on the PA Schools Work campaign and its increased focus on racial equity proposals, spurred on by nationwide protests in 2020 in the wake of the killings of George Floyd, Breonna Taylor, and many more, at the hands of the police. The chapter analyzes how the confluence of shifting membership within the coalition and increased public consciousness of racial injustices encouraged remaining members to emphasize race in its advocacy work and considers the wins that were achieved as a result. Drawing on the work of other school funding scholars, I offer a reparations framework of school funding to expand our thinking of what a serious investment in Black and Brown children might look like. I highlight the importance of movement-building in laying the groundwork for change as a necessary part of building the education systems our students of color deserve.

A final note: As I wrote this book, one of the audiences I had in mind were people who, like me and like many of the undergraduates I teach, care about issues of race and school funding but find the "weeds" of education policy less than scintillating. Financial facts and figures are unavoidable in a book about school funding. But at its heart, this is a story about how people in positions of power wield their structural power to maintain the racial school funding status quo, and how community organizers sought to contest white-district domination. My hope is that by keeping that narrative throughline in view, the technical details will be less of a slog.

### CHAPTER TWO

# Policies and Structures That Protect White-District Domination

As Rochelle Nichols-Solomon sat at my kitchen island, she registered her moral indignation with the Pennsylvania school funding policy known as "hold harmless." That day, she and a friend came over to brainstorm ways that I could be involved in POWER, an interfaith organizing group that has been working to eliminate racial bias in the state's allocation of school funding. Rochelle is a beloved elder in the progressive education community in Philadelphia, continuing a legacy of community activism passed down through her mother, Mamie Nichols—a matriarch of South Philadelphia who has been honored through affordable housing units named after her and a mural in Point Breeze that bears her likeness. Rochelle's Philadelphia roots run deep. Like many African Americans during the Great Migration, Mamie Nichols's family moved up north, from Virginia to Philadelphia, when she was an infant. Rochelle, along with her spouse, James, raised two children in Philadelphia and their grandchildren are fifth-generation Philadelphians who attend the city's public schools.

Rochelle's older daughter likes to describe her mom's twin passions in life as "RADICAL SCHOOL REFORM" and "home decor," adjusting the timbre of her voice to achieve maximum comic effect. That much was clear as Rochelle alternated between giving me home organizing advice—"You've got to use the space you already have"—and updating me on POWER's statewide education campaign. She told me that Representative Rabb's new bill, HB 961, proposed what POWER had been calling for all along: abolishing "hold harmless."

In Rochelle's estimation, "hold harmless" was a complete misnomer because it inflicted significant harm on majority-minority school districts like Philadelphia. She told me how she recently explained to her husband James that "hold harmless" is the main mechanism for maintaining racial disparities in state funding. Summoning James's incredulity, she reenacted his response, spitting out the words "hold harmless" like it was yesterday's coffee. Finishing her story, she said, "There's no 'hold harmless' when there's already harm done!"

The most damaging effects of the policy date back to 1992 when the Pennsylvania state legislature froze state education aid and uncoupled the distribution of state aid from student population. Rather than distributing state aid dynamically, according to a district's changing student enrollment, the policy guarantees that school districts receive at least as much as they received during a baseline year, regardless of increases or decreases to student enrollment. Because most of Pennsylvania's education aid to school districts is based on outdated population data from 1991 (McCorry 2016d), this method of distributing state aid does not recognize the growing financial needs of school districts with rising student populations. While this benefits white rural districts that have seen declines in their student populations since the 1990s by maintaining their funding levels (hence the term *hold harmless*), it comes at a significant cost to majority-minority urban districts, many of which have experienced growth in student enrollment since the 1990s but have not seen an increase in their revenues to reflect that growing enrollment. The policy has been redubbed *hold harmful* by POWER members because of the considerable harm it has caused majority-Black-and-Latine school districts across the state.

This chapter closely examines the policy of hold harmful to reveal how white-district domination became the default mode of school funding. I turn to the history of hold harmful in the 1980s and the policy decisions that created the dire financial conditions we see today. I situate these Pennsylvania policies within broader national policies that eroded welfare provisions while disparaging Black communities. Next, I examine hold harmful today, unpacking the flawed logic of Republican state lawmakers who argued that eliminating hold harmful and putting all the money through the fair funding formula was impossible because it created "winners and losers." I draw on quantitative data to show how the policy already created "winners and losers" by benefiting white districts. Protecting white districts that have experienced population loss was a colorblind trick of the trade used to defend the racially biased policy. Hold harmful was allowed to prevail because Republican lawmakers exploited the electoral structures that maintained their political power. The final section of this chapter shows how gerrymandering, and the system of winner-takes-all elections has unfairly tilted representation in favor of the Republican Party. Supported by electoral structures that give Republican legislators an unfair advantage, these lawmakers have, at every turn, firmly resisted transforming a racially inequitable system of school finance.

## DECADES OF HOLD HARMFUL

Hold harmful and the school funding precarity of today's majority-minority districts have historical antecedents. This section provides the origin stories of the hold harmful provision. Like other post–civil rights policies, attacks on the livelihoods of Black and Brown people have occurred through attacks on social spending and state provisions. Pennsylvania's 1983 Equalized Subsidy for Basic Education (ESBE) policy was part of an attack on education spending, which has exacted severe consequences to this day (for a timeline of major events, see appendix A). School funding advocates often recall, somewhat wistfully, that the ESBE formula was the last time the state distributed its funding in a way that actually accounted for numbers of students and for economic factors.[1] Despite the merits of that, ESBE should also be remembered for marking the end of the state's provision to fund 50 percent of the cost of public education—a decision that has had deleterious effects on the majority of Pennsylvania's Black and Brown students.

The 50 percent provision was enacted in 1966, following on the heels of a series of major national advancements in the struggle for Black liberation including the 1964 Civil Rights Act and the 1965 Voting Rights Act. But by 1983, the national stage had already provided several examples of how to employ colorblindness and racially coded language to chip away at the welfare state. Because of the success of the Civil Rights and Black Power movements of the 1960s, public expressions of racism were so significantly curtailed that even President Nixon, one of the chief architects of the "Southern strategy," was forced to disguise his racist sentiments under colorblind language. As Keeanga-Yamahtta Taylor (2016:63) observed:

> Where the Black movement had, as a result of protests and theorization, succeeded in defining racism as systemic and institutional, Nixon officials worked to narrow the definition of racism to the intentions of individual actors while countering the idea of institutional racism by focusing on 'freedom of choice' as a way to explain differential outcomes.

The language of "freedom of choice" conveniently exonerated racist policies of redlining and segregation, and "reduce[d] social inequality to individual behaviors" (Taylor 2016:70). This chastisement specifically targeted poor Black urbanites who were chided by Nixon's first secretary of Housing and Urban Development for their "bad habits, lawlessness, laziness, unemployment, inadequate education, low working skills, ill health, poor motivation and a negative self-image" (Darrow 1973).

If the Nixon administration laid the ideological groundwork for eroding social programs, it took "the swinging axe of Ronald Reagan to completely destroy the Johnson welfare state" (Taylor 2016:71). Reagan infamously introduced America to the fictitious and stereotypically racist social figures of the "strapping young buck" and "welfare queen," without ever having to mention race. As president, he gutted the budgets that provided social safety nets, including unemployment insurance, food stamps, Medicare, and jobs, and he raised rent for federally subsidized housing (Taylor 2016:93). The worst of these cuts were those aimed at children. In 1982, just a year before ESBE was passed, the federal school lunch program was reduced by $560 million, forcing 590,000 children to no longer receive what was, for some, their only meal of the day (Taylor 2016:93).

In 1983, riding on the coattails of successful cuts made to federal social programs, Pennsylvania, led by a Republican-controlled Senate and Republican governor, enacted their own laws that abdicated state responsibility for public education. Though the state did not technically "cut" its education budget, its removal of the 50 percent provision meant that localities have had to shoulder the burden of rising state mandated costs of education over the last four decades—that is, the costs of pension, special education, and charter school tuition. In 1971, the state contributed 54 percent toward the cost of education; by 2019, that figure was 32 percent (Bissett, Hillman, and Elliott 2019:61). For affluent suburban school districts that were able to make up the difference, the shift in financial burden had little to no effect on their educational programs. For financially struggling urban school districts, the removal of the 50 percent provision had ruinous consequences.

ESBE also included a hold harmful provision that was written into the 1983 law and its 1985 amendment, which exacerbated the inequities. The ESBE formula was created with the intention of providing a "rational" calculation of how much state aid districts should receive— that is, a calculation that was not haphazard and not based on politics, but rather based on factors like average daily attendance and district wealth. Theoretically, according to the ESBE formula, more state aid would go to districts with less local wealth, and less state aid would go to districts with more local wealth. But right out of the gate, the ESBE formula was undermined by hold harmful language. Perhaps as a compromise to the elimination of the 50 percent provision, the 1983 law stated that districts would receive at least 102 percent of what they received in the previous year (Bissett, Hillman, and Elliott 2019).

By 1985, ESBE contained not only a hold harmful minimum provision, but also a maximum cap (Bissett, Hillman, and Elliott 2019). According to the Pennsylvania Association of Rural and Small Schools (PARSS), "because ESBE contained artificial caps, both minimum and maximum caps, some school districts were being allocated more than 100 percent of what the ESBE formula generated and other districts were receiving far less than what the ESBE formula generated" (Bissett, Hillman, and Elliott 2019:25). In the following excerpt, PARSS provided more specific examples of how these artificial caps disadvantaged low-income districts:

> The combination of a minimum aid ratio of 15 percent for wealthy districts and yearly 2 percent increases regardless of changes in wealth and student population, provided some wealthy districts with more than 200 percent of their subsidy entitlement by the

1990–1991 school year.... The low income districts had the opposite problem. The result of caps of 6–8 percent on increases calculated by the formula resulted in many low income districts receiving far less than their entitlement. (Bissett, Hillman, and Elliott 2019:27)

With the introduction of artificial minimum and maximum caps, funding allocations were no longer strictly tied to district need, whether that need was based on number of students or district wealth. This delinking of allocation and district need was compounded over the ten years that ESBE and its artificial minimums and maximums were in use, leading to an increase in funding disparity and tax effort.

In 1992, despite booming national and state economies, the Pennsylvania legislature, with a Democratic-controlled House, a Democratic governor, and a split Senate, voted against increasing state education aid and froze funding allocations. The year 1992 has been described by school funding advocates as one in which the state took a "policy nosedive" (Public Citizens for Children and Youth 2021:8). Despite the cost of education rising by an average of 7 percent during this ten-year window, increases to the state's basic education funding was "0" in 1992, and "0" again in 1996 (Bissett, Hillman, and Elliott 2019:29).

Even more damaging, the state legislature froze the allocation of funding in 1992, which effectively meant that the ten "prior years of inequity [that were created through ESBE's artificial limits] were built into all future attempts to provide equity in funding" (Bissett, Hillman, and Elliott 2019:29). The artificial minimum and maximum payments "provided many districts with state funds which they would not have earned without these artificial components and denied many districts the additional funding earned if the formula had not been so constrained" (Bissett, Hillman, and Elliott 2019:29). During this time, earmarked funding was allocated to select districts that were financially struggling as a result of these policy decisions (Bissett, Hillman, and Elliott 2019:29). Earmarked funding, however, provided only a paper-thin cushion to mitigate the immense damage done to schools and students because of hold harmful and the frozen funding in 1992.

The 1990s was a bad decade for Pennsylvania students. First, hold harmful became the default education funding policy in 1992. Though Pennsylvania's school funding advocates frequently cite 1992 as the year that hold harmful was implemented, the language of hold harmful dates back to the 1983 act that implemented ESBE. However, in 1992, with state education aid frozen, the ESBE formula was no longer in play, which meant that hold harmful became the default method for distributing state education funds. In other words, while the ESBE years were damaging because artificial minimums and maximums undermined the integrity of the ESBE formula, allocations were at least partially based on a formula calculation that distributed state aid dynamically, according to the changing needs of districts. By 1992, there was no formula to speak of, and because hold harmful "became king" (McCorry 2016a), allocations were stagnantly determined, completely decoupled from district need. Philadelphia was specifically "hurt in the first few years of hold harmless, as it added tens of thousands of new students without any systematic acknowledgement from the state" (McCorry 2016d). When today's school funding advocates say that the inequity is "baked into the system," these are the policy decisions they are referring to.

Second, the 1990s ushered in an educational era that ramped up high-stakes testing in the name of "accountability" and "standards." The year 1992 was also when Pennsylvania launched its standardized test—the Pennsylvania System of School Assessment (PSSA). Taking a cue from the Nixon and Reagan administrations, so-called objective standardized test data could be mobilized to shame Black and Latine students for their presumed individual failings. This form of structural gaslighting allowed racist "culture-of-poverty" narratives that blamed the victim to flourish, while providing a colorblind cover for the terrible policy decisions of state lawmakers and the structural conditions that led to low test scores.

With hold harmful as the default means for allocating state aid to districts since 1992, funding inequity has continued to grow. From 1992 until 2016, with the exception of a three-year period from 2008 to 2011, Pennsylvania held the dubious distinction of being one of only three states in the nation that lacked a funding formula (McCorry 2016a). Although more than one-third of the state's 500 districts have either grown or contracted by more than 25 percent since 1991 (McCorry 2016a), state aid has remained incomprehensibly stagnant and has failed to keep pace with the changing needs of districts. According to one estimate, 53 percent of the state's basic education funding in 2014 can be traced back to outdated student enrollment data from 1990 (Mc-Corry 2016a). This stagnant approach toward distributing state aid has done the most harm to students of color, with 82 percent of the state's Black and Latine students attending a growing school district (Public Citizens for Children and Youth 2021:14) that has lost out in the game of school funding because of the policy of hold harmful.

Pennsylvania school funding policies have played out in ways that prevented cross-racial solidarity between poor districts. Poor districts serving students of all races suffered from the elimination of the 50 percent provision. This could have served as an opportunity for majority-white *and* majority-minority districts to work together and demand that the state provide sufficient funding for education. Yet this would not be so. As we know now, the effects of hold harmful were anything but colorblind, benefiting mostly poor white rural districts and disadvantaging mostly poor urban majority-minority school districts. According to the Education Law Center (2017:18), the fifty whitest districts in Pennsylvania (with an average of 99 percent white students) received about $10,000 per student from the state, while the least white districts (with an average of only 38 percent white students) received about $7,000 per student from the state, for a difference of $3,000 per student. White-district domination was maintained through the colorblind policies of artificial caps, freezing education aid, and hold harmful. The next section examines hold harmful today—that is, the flawed logics of lawmakers in defending hold harmful and the racially biased effects on school districts.

## HAMSTRINGING THE 2016 FAIR FUNDING FORMULA

On a muggy day in late September, my students and I met with David Mosenkis, a bespectacled man with salt and pepper hair, to talk about his work with POWER. As we swatted away mosquitoes beneath a lush tree canopy, David told us about how he got involved in issues of school funding through his synagogue, a member organization in POWER. He explained that "POWER looks at all of its work through a lens of race and understanding that systemic and structural racism permeates all the systems that we're trying to make changes in." At the time of the interview, David had published two important reports (Mosenkis 2014;

Mosenkis 2016) that demonstrated the prevalence of racial bias in the state's distribution of basic education funding. Rochelle has often said that David's quantitative findings "put the wind in POWER's sails" and catalyzed its campaign for fair education funding. As he put it, "we've helped raise the visibility of this issue that was hidden." I simply refer to David as a *bad-ass data scientist.*

Surprisingly, David went on to explain that the data for demonstrating Pennsylvania's racial school funding gap "was always there. It's not really hard to find. I didn't do some kind of groundbreaking type of new research to discover this. Anybody could've, if they dug into the numbers, found this pattern of racial bias." The main difference between POWER and other groups involved in school funding was that POWER was asking questions about racial disparities, while most other groups were not; POWER saw its work as actively dismantling systemic racism, while most others did not. David's comments underscore a simple, yet important point for those who subscribe to colorblind logics: ignoring race doesn't make racism go away.

In 2016, POWER organizers held out hope that things would take a real turn for the better. The Basic Education Funding (BEF) Commission was a bipartisan, bicameral group of fifteen state legislators tasked with developing a school funding formula for distributing state aid. Many advocates felt that the commission's work was long overdue since a student-weighted formula had not been in use since 1992, except for the three-year period (2008–2011) during Governor Rendell's tenure. The formula developed by the BEF Commission received widespread praise for how it fairly accounted for factors including wealth, number of students, levels of poverty, number of English learners, charter school enrollment, and geographic sparsity. This gave rise to the formula being referred to as the "fair funding formula."

POWER's celebration over the fair funding formula was short-lived. Though the state legislature adopted the formula, there was an asterisk attached to their decision: the formula would only be applied to *increases* in state education aid. The lion's share of the state education budget would continue to be distributed according to the hold harmful provision that included decades of known inequities. The first year that the 2016 fair funding formula was used, only 3 percent of Pennsylvania's $5.6 billion education budget was distributed "fairly"—that is, driven through the new formula (McCorry 2016b). In 2021, with further increases to the state's basic education funding pot, that figure stood at 11 percent (Public Citizens for Children and Youth 2021). As Kevin McCorry (2016c), a Pennsylvania education reporter noted, "A school funding formula is only as good as the money that goes through it."

State legislators frequently tried to justify their 2016 decision by arguing that putting all the money through the fair funding formula would create "winners and losers." A retired state representative who was sympathetic to eliminating hold harmful explained, "Any proposal that would have winners and losers . . . is not likely to happen in the General Assembly. [As an] intellectual argument, it absolutely ought to be done. It would be more fair. In a practical political world, not likely to happen." While sympathetic to issues of fairness, this representative nevertheless voiced a common bias among state legislators: that eliminating hold harmful would *create* "winners and losers." This perspective ignores that the 2016 decision didn't avoid the creation of "winners and losers"; it reinforced existing "winners and losers."

David Mosenkis's 2016 report provided a new analysis of racial bias in Pennsylvania school funding. The publication was released just one month after Governor Wolf signed into law the fair funding formula, with the provision to preserve hold harmful and all the racial inequities that have been built into it. The timing of the report was not coincidental. Though legislators claim that the 2016 decision avoided the creation of "winners and losers," his report demonstrated the fallacy of this statement. According to the following scatter plot graph (figure 1) found in the report, districts serving more students of color tend to receive less than they would have if all the money ran through the fair funding formula.

The line of best fit (dashed line) represents the ideal, where actual funding levels are equivalent to having 100 percent of basic education run through the formula. Districts that are above the line are funded at levels above the formula-calculated amount, while districts below the line are funded at levels below the formula calculation.

A distinct pattern emerges among the dots, which represent each of Pennsylvania's five hundred districts: dots above the line (i.e., districts that receive more than the formula calculation) are overwhelmingly lighter colored (denoting a high share of white students), whereas the

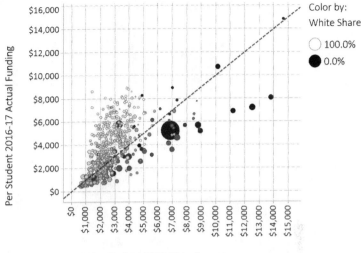

*Figure 1.* Racial inequities in Pennsylvania's basic education funding. This scatter plot graph shows the relationship between the percentage of white students in a district and how much per-pupil funding they receive, relative to their "fair share." From David Mosenkis's 2016 report.

dots below the line tend to be darker colored (denoting a low share of white students). The size of the dots is proportionate to the number of students in a district. The largest dot in the graph represents the School District of Philadelphia, which in 2019–2020 educated about 12 percent of the total number of students in Pennsylvania public schools and has a white share of only 14 percent (Pennsylvania Department of Education, Data Collection Team 2021). If 100 percent of basic education funding were funneled through the fair funding formula, Philadelphia students would receive about $7,000 per pupil. However, because of the hold harmful provision, Philadelphia only receives about $5,000 per pupil—$2,000 less than its fair share per pupil. In total, in 2019, the School District of Philadelphia (SDP), received about $400 million less than it would have if all the money ran through the formula. Many other smaller cities have also been cheated out of their fair share as a result of hold harmful.

Figure 2, produced by the Pennsylvania House Appropriations

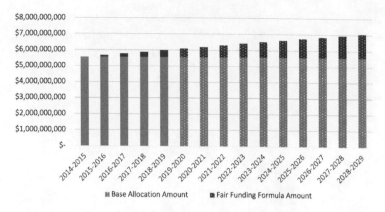

*Figure 2*. Incremental effects of preserving hold harmful. This bar graph shows the incremental effects of putting only new money through the fair funding formula while maintaining a policy of hold harmful. Produced by the Pennsylvania House Appropriations Committee (D).

Committee, demonstrates the effects of the state legislature's decision over a fifteen-year period. The lighter gray bars indicate the base amount of education subsidies (solid bars represent actual allocations, and patterned bars represent projected allocations), while the darker gray bars represent the new money put into the education funding that is distributed according to the fair funding formula. By their own account, if $100 million were added to the basic education subsidy every year, it would take nearly a decade and a half, from the time the formula was first introduced, before only 22 percent (or $1.54 billion of the $7.1 billion education budget) was distributed fairly. The retired representative I spoke with put it in more personal terms: "My middle granddaughter is now seventeen . . . if we continue to apply the new formula at the current pace, which is barely more than $100 million a year, [my granddaughter] will be sixty-five years old . . . when we get to the point where even half of the money going out is distributed through this new formula."

The delay of justice is a familiar and effective tactic for maintaining racial hierarchy. People in power use it to try to appease dissident voices; to claim they are "making progress." Pennsylvania state legislators claim that these "baby steps" are necessary and point to the creation of a fair funding formula as proof of "progress." But rather than the narrative of "progress," the actions of state legislators offer a stark example of what Dr. King said: "For years now I have heard the word 'Wait!' It rings in the ear of every Negro with piercing familiarity. This 'Wait' has almost always meant 'Never.' We must come to see . . . that 'justice too long delayed is justice denied'" (King 1963).

## HOLD HARMFUL AND POPULATION CHANGE

The delay of justice and the persistence of racial bias in Pennsylvania school funding today are achieved through the race-neutral justification that districts with population decline need a financial safety net. Strong patterns emerge when examining the relationship between student enrollment, district inequities, and race. The map (figure 3) "Student enrollment change, 1990–2020" illustrates population change over the course of three decades. As the map demonstrates, population decline (as indicated in white) has occurred throughout Pennsylvania, but mostly in the central and western part of the state, in rural areas that

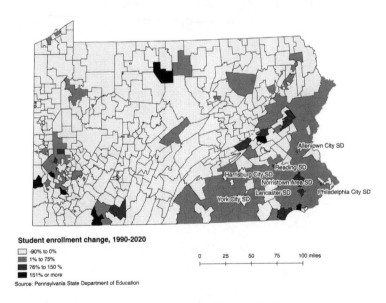

**Student enrollment change, 1990-2020**

☐ -90% to 0%
▨ 1% to 75%
■ 76% to 150 %
■ 151% or more

0    25    50    75    100 miles

Source: Pennsylvania State Department of Education

*Figure 3.* Changing student enrollment. Increases and decreases in student population from 1990 to 2020 in Pennsylvania school districts. Map by Alisha Butler and Amy Hillier.

experienced the decline of the steel, coal, and textile industries (Public Citizens for Children and Youth 2021:10). The report *Hold "Harmless": A Quarter Century of Inequity at the Heart of Pennsylvania's School System,* by Public Citizens for Children and Youth (2021:10) makes a similar point by examining changing enrollment in school districts over a twenty-seven-year period. In contrast, student population growth (as indicated by varying shades of gray) has mostly occurred in the southeastern part of the state. The greatest increase in student enrollment (the darkest gray shade) has often occurred within "third-class cities" of Pennsylvania—that is, cities with less than 250,000 people—as companies in manufacturing, food processing, health care, and education have continued to attract and employ newer residents.

The next map, "Inequity in total dollars 2019–2020" (figure 4), shows what school districts are actually allocated in relation to their fair funding calculation. The white shade represents districts that receive between $1 to $79 million over their fair funding formula calculation, while the gray shades receive under their fair funding calculation. The darker the shade the greater the inequity, in total dollars. Again, the white-shaded areas are concentrated in the central and western parts of

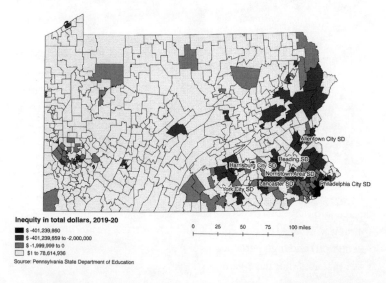

**Inequity in total dollars, 2019-20**
- ■ $ -401,239,860
- ■ $ -401,239,859 to -2,000,000
- ■ $ -1,999,999 to 0
- □ $1 to 78,614,936

Source: Pennsylvania State Department of Education

0   25   50   75   100 miles

*Figure 4.* Total school district funding inequities. Pennsylvania school districts receiving more or less than their "fair share." Map by Alisha Butler and Amy Hillier.

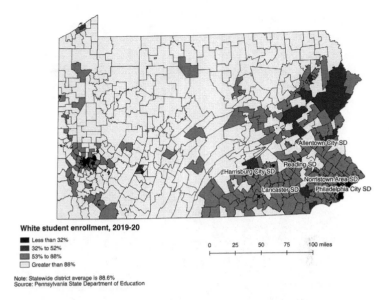

**White student enrollment, 2019-20**

- Less than 32%
- 32% to 52%
- 53% to 88%
- Greater than 88%

0    25    50    75    100 miles

Note: Statewide district average is 88.6%
Source: Pennsylvania State Department of Education

*Figure 5.* School district racial demographics. Percentages of white students in Pennsylvania school districts. Map by Alisha Butler and Amy Hillier.

the state, while the darker-shaded areas are focused along the eastern regions of the state. In comparing the two maps, we see that districts with population growth are also the districts that receive less than their fair funding calculation and have suffered the most under hold harmful.

The third and final map (figure 5), "White student enrollment, 2019–2020," illustrates the racial demographics of Pennsylvania's school districts. The highest percentage of white student enrollment (as indicated in white) tends to be in the central and western parts of the state, while the greatest percentages of students of color tend to be along the eastern part of Pennsylvania.

Looking at this series of three maps together, there is a strong relationship between changing student population, school funding inequity, and race. Districts that have lost students tend to have school funding windfalls (i.e., receiving more than their fair funding formula calculation) and high percentages of white students. The reverse is also true: districts that have gained students tend to be shortchanged in school funding (i.e., receiving less than their fair funding formula calculation) and educate higher percentages of students of color. White-

*Figure 6.* Triptych of maps. The relationship between changes in student enrollment (left), inequities in the distribution of state aid (middle), and percentages of white students (right). Maps by Alisha Butler and Amy Hillier.

district domination has been maintained through the race-neutral policy of protecting districts that have declining populations.

## GERRYMANDERING, PARTISAN GEOGRAPHIES, AND SCHOOL FUNDING INEQUITIES

The ability for Republican leaders to reflexively protect hold harmful is aided by gerrymandering and partisan geographies in the electoral process. Gerrymandering—the process of redrawing political districts on a map in a way that favors one party over others—has given Republican leaders immense and disproportionate power over rank-and-file members and the power to stymie any efforts to change the racial school funding status quo. Carol Kuniholm, a cofounder of Fair Districts PA, which works to "create a process for redistricting that is transparent, impartial and fair," became interested in gerrymandering by way of equitable school funding issues. A white woman with a gleaming head of gray hair, Kuniholm's unfussy appearance, easy smile, and slightly self-deprecating humor immediately put my students and me at ease as we listened to her explain how gerrymandering impedes equitable school funding.

Kuniholm was a former youth pastor and became interested in school funding issues when her church in Paoli (a predominantly white, affluent suburb of Philadelphia) partnered with a school in Kensington, North Philly—a racially diverse working-class neighborhood of Black, white, Latine, and Asian residents, known for its steel and textile manufacturing through the nineteenth and twentieth centuries. Because of deindustrialization, the local economy began to decline in the 1950s, and Kensington became known for its open-air drug markets by the

1970s. As Kuniholm reflected on the differences between the school in Paoli and the school in Kensington, she was struck by the stark contrast in resources. Paoli kids, she said, "went to a school that had an indoor swimming pool, and they went on school trips to Europe. . . . I went to see their school plays and every single kid had one of those nice little lapel microphones." Kensington kids "did not have a school library, did not have school counselors. They did not have a school auditorium. And I just thought, 'There's something super messed up here.'"

With the clarity and storytelling flair of someone who is used to talking to teens, Kuniholm explained how she was puzzled and frustrated by the intransigence of the state legislature. "Nothing changes. Nothing budges. Nothing moves," she said reproachingly. She told us that as she dug deeper into the root causes of why "nothing changes," she realized that gerrymandering was a big part of the problem. As she put it: "Gerrymandering gives legislators a safe district; . . . as long as they hold on to their safe district, they don't have to listen to you [the constituents]; they have to listen to the [party] leaders. The leaders are the ones who draw the maps. . . . The leaders control everything." In other words, because party leaders control how the map is drawn, and because leaders can manipulate the district boundaries in ways that support or imperil rank-and-file legislators' election outcomes, your everyday state legislator is at the mercy of party leaders. The partisan process of redistricting is a highly effective tool for disciplining rank-and-file members to toe the political line. If they remain in the good graces of party leaders, they can continue to "hold on to their safe district."

Many people I spoke with pointed to Mike Turzai, the former Speaker of the House, as someone who embodied this partisanship. Turzai wielded control over his caucus and had an outsized influence over the legislature. Kuniholm talked about how the shale tax in Pennsylvania could have increased funding for public education, but it wasn't even allowed to come to a vote because Speaker Turzai blocked it. She said:

> There's something really broken in the legislative process when one person like that, one idealogue [Mike Turzai] with his own opinions can detonate the whole thing. He's one representative. There's

203 representatives. So he is less than half of 1 percent of the state. Less than half of 1 percent of the state is controlling the budget, controlling the legislative process. . . . It's not good. That's not . . . the way it's supposed to work.

But because of gerrymandering, a political culture of partisanship, and the outsized influence of the Speaker of the House, that *is* how it worked. Though Speaker Turzai was only 1 out of 203 representatives, his famously low regard for public education "controll[ed] the budget, controll[ed] the legislative process." Having redistricting in his back pocket allowed him to hold on to this power.

Redistricting is a process in which congressional and state legislative districts are redrawn every ten years. Whichever political party is in power draws the maps in their party's favor. Redrawing Pennsylvania's legislative districts is dictated by a commission of five people: the House majority leader; the House minority leader; the Senate majority leader; the Senate minority leader; and a person appointed by the state supreme court. In 2011, the last time the redistricting process occurred, Pennsylvania Republicans not only enjoyed a trifecta (controlling the state House, Senate, and governorship), the state supreme court (whose justices are elected) was also majority Republican. The Republican Party attempted to parlay these political winnings into future winnings by redrawing the maps in their favor. Though Pennsylvania's *congressional* maps received a great deal of media attention and was the center of a 2018 lawsuit that showed that Republicans had egregiously manipulated the maps, it is important to note that several challenges were also issued against the state's 2011 *legislative* maps. According to experts, when the same computer-based techniques used in the 2018 congressional maps case were applied to the legislative maps, it showed that "the [legislative] maps skew toward Republicans, and that it is unlikely this happened organically" (Albiges 2021).

*Packing* and *cracking* are gerrymandering methods by which electoral boundaries are manipulated to secure as many seats as possible for the party in power. "Packing crams voters of the rival party into a few districts to give that party overwhelming wins. Cracking spreads members of the rival party across a large number of districts so their votes don't matter as much" (Albiges 2021). As it relates to the 2011 maps for

Pennsylvania, it meant that Democratic votes were distributed ineffi-
ciently and had many more "wasted" votes, either because it *packed*
Democratic voters together so the party yielded many more votes than
were needed to win, or it *cracked* Democratic votes so that they were
in districts that were narrowly won by Republican candidates. In the
2018 elections for state senate, which used the 2011 legislative maps that
were approved by a Republican-controlled commission, Republicans
won their districts by an average of 64.4 percent of votes, whereas
Democrats won by an average of 69.9 percent of votes (Albiges 2021).
According to the Princeton Gerrymandering Project, "the chance that
this 5 percent difference would have arisen by 'nonpartisan processes
alone' is almost zero" (Albiges 2021).

While gerrymandering provides an important explanation for why
Republicans have had a stronghold on state politics, urbanization and
the creation of partisan geographies provides another explanation
for why the efficiency gap is a particularly Democratic problem. In
*Why Cities Lose*, Jonathan Rodden (2019) explains that industrial cities
were designed around waterways, natural resources, and transporta-
tion nodes and facilitated a concentration of laborers around factories
and housing complexes. As time passed, "The party that emerged as
a champion of urban workers during the New Deal morphed into the
party of post-industrial cities and towns" (Rodden 2019:48). Pennsylvania's cities exemplify the partisan geographies that emerged from this
urban industrial history: a Democratic urban core and a Republican
periphery. "In Allentown, as in Reading, one must travel only 5 kilometers to go from 80 percent Democratic precincts to a ring of evenly
divided precincts. And in another 5 kilometers, one is already in the
staunchly Republican periphery, with an average Republican vote share
of around 60 percent" (Rodden 2019:107).

Because Republicans are more evenly dispersed across the state
compared to Democratic voters, who tend to be concentrated in cities, Republicans have less wasted votes. Rodden argues that cities lose
when this "type of geographic polarization is combined with an old-
fashioned system of winner-take-all electoral districts like the one in
the United States" (2019:10). In electoral systems that are based on
proportional representation, wasted votes are a nonissue. Partisan polarization is most intense in states like Pennsylvania with postindustrial

cities that have small Democratic urban cores and large Republican peripheries.

Gerrymandering and partisan geographies in Pennsylvania have given Republican state legislators the political advantage. They have used that power to consistently stonewall any efforts to change the state's school funding scheme, unwilling to even bring the issue of eliminating hold harmful to the table for a vote. Cloaked under the colorblind guises of freezing education aid and population change, hold harmful has served as a policy that protects white-district domination. When electoral structures, like gerrymandering and a winner-takes-all system give Republican Party leaders such substantial and disproportionate power, then the interests of various constituents do not compete on an even playing field. Republican leaders have consistently used their power to protect white rural districts, at the expense of urban school districts serving predominantly Black and Latine students.

As the next chapter shows, because of the damaging effects of hold harmful, stopgap efforts were necessary to stanch the severe financial deprivation of majority-minority districts. Within the Pennsylvania state legislature, senior leaders from both parties made it a habit to dole out pork barrel money as a way of forcing its party members to toe the party line. Earmarked school funding was one of these pork barrel practices. School districts were cherry-picked to receive earmarked school funding to boost legislators' chances at reelection and maintain political power. While most of the districts that received earmarked funds were majority-minority and desperately needed the infusion of money, chapter 3 contends that these stopgap efforts prevented systemic overhaul of the school funding system.

### CHAPTER THREE

# Stopgap Efforts for a Systemic Problem

In 2013, the *LNP*, one of Lancaster's daily newspapers, broke the following story: "Legislators Give $30.3 M to 21 School Districts behind Closed Doors" (Hawkes 2013). Despite the fiscal impropriety suggested by the headline, the Senate majority leader insisted that these districts were selected to receive earmarked funding because they met "financial stress benchmarks" (Hawkes 2013). Most of these twenty-one school districts served a student body that was majority-minority and largely poor (according to eligibility for free or reduced lunch). The infusion of money helped put these struggling districts on more stable financial grounds (Education Law Center 2013b) and provided a modicum of relief from the larger racial injustice of inadequate and inequitable funding.

Yet seen from the critical race prism of interest-convergence, earmarked school funding to districts of color was possible because it aligned with the interests of predominantly white lawmakers: reelection. David Mayhew (2004) has argued that politicians' behaviors are largely driven by the desire to get reelected, or what he refers to as "the electoral incentive." Politicians are incentivized to focus on things that lead to reelection, like being able to claim credit for something, or taking a position that is favorable to constituents. For state lawmakers, earmarked funding was a means for reelection. It gave them the appearance of being on the right side of school funding and allowed them to claim credit for securing funding for their constituents. Since constituents rarely follow the vagaries of school funding policies, it mattered little that earmarked funding was a poorly constructed stopgap effort for a systemic problem. The triumphant press releases got the job done. For the state legislature's senior leadership, having the ability to dole out discretionary money like earmarked funding also served their interest of consolidating power. It was a carrot and a stick to keep rank-and-file members in line and whip up the votes needed on other issues.

This chapter demonstrates the tricks of the trade that legislators used to selectively funnel money into their districts to bolster their chances for reelection. These tricks of the trade included the use of hyper-specific language that only applied to one district, moving earmarked funds from one line item to another to evade detection, and the simple yet effective practice of party leaders who played by their own set of rules. While earmarked funding was welcome news to cash-strapped districts, it maintained the racial school funding gap by undermining efforts to build the organizing power necessary to *systemically* address the state's perennial misfunding of school districts. "Justice is not a natural part of the lifecycle of the United States, nor is it a product of evolution; it is always the outcome of struggle" (Taylor 2016:5). Earmarked funding dampened the impulse to engage in a collective struggle to eradicate systemic racism in school funding. It had a smoke-and-mirrors effect that gave constituents the false sense that they were getting what they needed and that their state legislators were doing their jobs. It is a practice that placates our sense of justice, making us willing to accept the scraps of school funding provided and to concede to the racial school funding status quo.

## PENNSYLVANIA'S POLITICAL CULTURE OF PAROCHIALISM AND PARTISANSHIP

A political culture of parochialism and partisanship permeated Pennsylvania's General Assembly and explains why earmarked funding thrived. When I interviewed Republican and Democratic state legislators, I asked what the biggest impediments were to eliminating hold harmful. Invariably, they presented it as a "numbers" or "math" problem: you could never get enough politicians to vote against the interests of their own constituents, who were currently benefiting from the policy. As one state legislator stated:

> You still need 102 votes in the House and 26 in the Senate to get a school funding formula to the governor's desk for a signature. And

that requires, you know, being cognizant of the fact that members will be protective of the funding they can bring home to their districts.

While this dynamic is not unique to Pennsylvania, the state's political culture fostered a particularly self-interested style of governance that neglected the collective good.

When one of my students asked a Lehigh Valley legislator what he thought the biggest hurdle was to passing equitable school funding policies, he characterized Pennsylvania politics as "parochial."

> Well, it kind of gets back to the point I made about when the spread-sheets come out on school funding. All the members race to the caucus room to see how their districts did. The biggest hurdles tend to be on the political side of things. You can make a very, very strong rational argument for having a formula. . . . The problem you run into is that most legislators, whether they're senators or represen-tatives, tend to take a very parochial view, making sure that their districts receive funding at least at a hold harmless level.

A "strong rational argument" does not carry the day when it comes to Pennsylvania politics. This was a sentiment repeated in numerous inter-views I had with people who worked in Harrisburg. Instead, the political instinct was to "race to the caucus room to see how *their* districts did . . . making sure that *their* districts receive funding at least at a hold harmless level" (italics added), even if there were other districts with greater needs.

This parochialism was baked into the wheeling and dealings of Har-risburg politics and codified into a category of money earmarked for individual legislators; the practice was so common that it had its own acronym: WAM. When I first heard the acronym from a Philadelphia rep-resentative, I needed clarification. "WAM?" I asked. Responding matter-of-factly, he said, "Walk-around-money—a pot of money that you could somehow get a hold of that could benefit your district at the expense of others." WAMs were not limited to spending on school districts. Rather, it was a broad use of discretionary money (a.k.a. pork barrel spending) controlled by legislative leaders who negotiated the budget. In turn, lead-ers awarded WAMs to those who voted according to their directives. WAMs helped incumbents get reelected by allowing them to pursue pet projects that would increase their popularity among voters. These discretionary funds have been curtailed in the last decade because, as the Philadelphia representative explained, "it was felt that the process was unfair." Nevertheless, WAMs were a method used to control rank-and-file members and whip up the votes needed on a particular issue. Its long-standing practice is indicative of a quid-pro-quo Harrisburg culture.

If naked self-interest was one facet of the political culture in Harrisburg, blind adherence to party leaders was another. I spoke with a Democratic staffer, Dan, who explained this process in detail. Like many state legislators and staffers, Dan is a white man of Generation X and dressed in a style of clothing that was birthed in Silicon Valley in the 1980s and given the name "business casual." *Business casual* also captured his affective expression—relaxed but focused. He was refreshingly candid in answering my questions. In response to my question about why the 2016 BEF Commission went through all the trouble of developing a new formula, when Governor Rendell already had a formula in place from 2011, Dan said it was partisan rancor—an effort to undo the work of the Democratic governor—led by Republican Party leaders and adhered to by rank-and-file legislators.

> No one could get anything moved that had the word "Rendell" attached to it. . . . And so immediately after the formula was adopted under Rendell, you had Republican leadership trashing the formula. And so they then poisoned the well for any new members coming in. . . . It was such a . . . campaign to discredit it that even legislators who were benefiting from the formula didn't take the time to really look at it because they were told by their leaders that it was bad. So they had no knowledge of it actually helping their school districts. They were just told it was bad and they accepted that as truth. And so if you were to talk to them, they would just say, "Oh, that's bad," even if you showed them a spreadsheet that it helped them. And it just, you know, it is indicative, and I apologize for veering so much into the politics of this, but it's just so indicative of the mentality and the structure that exists in that building and the kind of lack of critical thinking that goes on.

This "lack of critical thinking" worked in favor of Republican leaders who could manipulate rank-and-file members to vote along party lines.

According to Dan, some members "didn't take the time to really look at it," but simply accepted what party leaders told them as truth. If they were told by party leaders that the formula was "bad," it was bad. No amount of logic or evidence—"even if you showed them a spreadsheet that [the formula] helped [their district]"—could convince them otherwise. One retired Democratic legislator who served for over two decades said, "The whole [legislative] process itself doesn't necessarily lend itself to high-level intellectual discussion on a particular proposal." Earmarked funding was an outgrowth of the state legislature's parochial and partisan style of governance, with funds distributed to improve reelection chances, to maintain power for a particular party, and to consolidate power for party leaders.

## PUTTING A BAND-AID ON A DISEASE

The distribution of earmarked funding had less to do with the actual needs of school districts than with politics. Because of this, earmarked funding didn't follow rhyme or reason. Districts that one might expect to receive earmarked funding were left empty handed, and districts with students who had greater needs received less earmarked funding. The comparative case of the School District of Lancaster (SDL) and the Harrisburg School District highlights this point. SDL received earmarked funding and was an example of a school district under financial stress. Receiving the fourth highest amount of earmarked funding ($2.4 million), 81 percent of Lancaster students qualified for free or reduced lunch (Education Law Center 2013a), 18 percent identified as students with Limited English Proficiency (Education Law Center 2013a), and 76 percent were Latine and Black students (Pennsylvania Department of Education, Data Collection Team 2021). In the years preceding 2013, SDL was forced to lay off twelve people in the central office, institute two years of spending and pay freezes, eliminate its elementary Spanish program, and gut its library staff. Despite these cuts to programs and staff, the *LNP* ran a headline in 2013 describing SDL as "financially thriving." The headline read: "Why the School District of Lancaster Is Financially Thriving When Similar Districts in Pennsylvania Are Failing" (Wallace 2013).

Lancaster schools could only be described as "financially thriving" when compared to other urban school districts facing far more desperate financial straits. In that article, Harrisburg was cited as worse off than Lancaster because it had been identified as "financially distressed" by the state and under financial watch. "Harrisburg," the article stated, "has amassed $437 million in debt and faces drastic cuts in personnel and programs" (Wallace 2013). Ninety-nine percent of Harrisburg students face poverty, 11 percent identify as LEP (Education Law Center 2013a), and 84 percent identified as nonwhite (Pennsylvania Department of Education, Data Collection Team 2013). Yet oddly, the Harrisburg School District did not receive earmarked funding in 2013.

Unlike most school districts that received earmarked funds, Harrisburg did not have a representative or senator who occupied a position of senior leadership in the state legislature. Ronald Cowell, former state representative and longtime advocate of school funding, commented that when only a select few school districts receive extra help behind closed doors, "we're left to conclude it was only a political process" (Hawkes 2013). An analysis of earmarked funding confirmed critics' suspicions: the allocation of educational money was tied to political connections. According to *The Philadelphia Public School Notebook*, "of the 37 lawmakers representing the districts that benefited from extra aid, 33 are majority/minority committee chairs, vice chairs, secretaries or in some other leadership position" (Socolar 2013). Moreover, $22 million of the total $30 million went to "areas represented by eight of the highest-ranking lawmakers in the General Assembly" (Socolar 2013). Distribution of earmarked funding rewarded school districts with high-ranking state legislators. The business manager for the Columbia School District—a financially struggling district that did not receive earmarked funding—commented, "Something's broken somewhere, and the system needs to be reviewed" (Hawkes 2013). A representative of the Upper Darby school district, which received earmarked funding in 2018, summed it up by saying that the "gift . . . isn't really a gift: It's penance for the lousy job [legislators are] doing in funding our district" (Tustin 2018).

The case of the School District of Lancaster demonstrates that earmarked funding acted as a temporary life preserver and did nothing to systematically improve the conditions of underfunded schools. In 2014, only one year after SDL received $2.4 million in earmarked funding, it joined with five other districts, six parents, and two statewide organizations as plaintiffs in the landmark lawsuit—*William Penn School District et al. v. PA Department of Education*—alleging that the state violated its constitutional duty to provide students with a basic education because of inadequate and inequitable funding. In the complaint Pedro Rivera, then-superintendent of SDL, attested to the cost-cutting measures they had to take because of insufficient funding:

> Lancaster has eliminated over 100 teaching positions and over 20 administrative staff positions, resulting in both larger class sizes and reductions in specialized personnel (e.g., technology coaches, and world language teachers). In Lancaster, the furniture is in poor condition, with desks, chairs, tables, and labs in need of repair or replacement. Many of the projectors are broken or need replacement bulbs, and many of the desktop computers are more than five years old, making them technologically obsolete. . . . Some schools in the district have had to ration paper in order to make their supply last through the end of the year. (Education Law Center 2014)

If this is what a "financially thriving" school district looks like, one shudders to consider the picture for districts deemed "financially distressed." To be "financially thriving," SDL had to not only trim the fat, but cut through bone. Small amounts of earmarked funding given to school districts neglected to address a problem that was, at its core, structural.

In my interview with Ronald Cowell, former state representative and longtime school funding advocate, he explained the problem of earmarked funding in the following way: "To the extent that those earmarked systems get used, they threaten to further delay the implementation of a more rational system, like putting Band-Aids on a wound and walking away rather than doing the major surgery that's necessary." Similarly, Rep. Mike Sturla, who represented the School District of Lancaster (SDL), criticized the legislature for its stopgap approach to school funding, even though SDL received the fourth highest amount of earmarked funding in 2013. "Lancaster County legislators don't need to get better at 'playing the game.' They need to start demanding a fair and equitable formula," Sturla said.

In 2013, when news broke about earmarked funding, Pennsylvania was still three years away from adopting a fair funding formula. Sturla's comment underscored his belief that the rules of "the [earmarked funding] game" were unfairly stacked against some school districts and that Pennsylvania legislators should not be content with dribs and drabs of earmarked funding. Instead, they should engage in the hard work of adopting and using a fair funding formula to address a systemic problem. For comparison's sake, while SDL received $2.4 million in earmarked funding in 2013, if all the money were routed through the 2016 fair funding formula, it would receive $25 million more every year.

If we see racist school-funding structures as a disease, and lack of resources in school districts as symptoms of that disease, then earmarked funding acted as a sloppily adhered Band-Aid that only applied to some ailing parts of the body and not others. Republican leaders, who have been in control of the state legislature for the better part of eight decades (Rodden 2019:156) and have stymied efforts to transform the school funding system, are analogous to negligent doctors who are satisfied with mitigating some symptoms, while neglecting to find a cure for the disease.

## PARTY LEADERS USE EARMARKED FUNDING TO DISCIPLINE RANK-AND-FILE LEGISLATORS

Earmarked funding facilitated blind adherence to party leaders and was an important tool that party leaders used to get the votes they needed. The lack of transparency of earmarked funding was intentional. Republican Senate Majority Leader Dominic Pileggi admitted, "If you're thinking there is an application form to participate, that's not how the process works" (Hawkes 2013). Instead, "the process" involved high-ranking legislators using their position to advocate for their districts. Democratic Representative Mike Schlossberg, whose Allentown School District was also represented by Republican Pat Browne, the fourth-highest-ranking state senator, took credit for Allentown's $8 million earmarked funding in 2013 saying, "Senator Browne and I each worked our separate parties and chambers, in a bipartisan manner and with shared passion, to get this done" (Hawkes 2013).

Representative Schlossberg's boast of bipartisanship is belied by the fact that "only two of the twenty-one school districts [that received earmarked funding] have no Republicans among their legislators" (Socolar 2013). Earmarked funding heavily skewed toward Republican-represented districts. However, what was bipartisan was the fact that both Democrats and Republicans engaged in the practice of earmarking funds to their own districts whenever their party was in power. Andrew Dinniman, Democratic state senator who represented Chester County, remarked: "Who gets the money often depends on the party in power, often depends on factors that are political. . . . If anything in this budget should be above politics, it should be our formula through which we give money to our schools" (Socolar 2013). But because the practice of earmarked funding offered huge political payoffs for Republicans and Democrats, school funding was not at all above politics. Pennsylvania's parochial and partisan culture not only tolerated, but in fact incentivized short-term fixes like earmarked funding.

When Democrats were given the chance to leverage their power to transform the school funding system in the early 1990s, they instead opted to continue the piecemeal practice of earmarked funding. A longtime state legislator suggested that earmarked funding was so built into the system that Democratic leaders, Representative Dwight Evans and Senator Vince Fumo, both of whom represented Philadelphia, "would not have been doing their jobs if they didn't get some extra money for Philadelphia" during the Democratic Party's "heyday" in the state legislature. Senator Pileggi admitted that earmarked funding was not the best way to do things, "but that is the only way that it's been done for at least a generation in Harrisburg, maybe two generations" (Hawkes 2013).

From 1991 to 1994, Dwight Evans was majority chair of the House Appropriations Committee (the committee that sets the agenda for how much money to appropriate and how to allocate it) and Vince Fumo was minority chair of the Senate Appropriations Committee. From 1995 to 2006, though Evans and Fumo had less influence, they still held substantial power as minority chairs of their respective appropriations committees. When I suggested that the early 1990s were the "heyday" for Philadelphia in terms of earmarked funding, the longtime legislator agreed saying, "You had it right, I guess, the 'heyday.' Yes. You had . . . two powerful legislators, House and Senate. Dwight was usually in the majority or certainly often. Vince, even when he was in the minority, was a huge influence. So that was a heyday. Yes." Despite a three-year window of near-peak political power for Philadelphia, and an eleven-year time frame of considerable power, Evans and Fumo spent the heyday years securing earmarked funding for Philadelphia schools instead of working to systematically change the racial school funding status quo.

Democratic leaders used earmarked funding to discipline their party. A state representative who has served in the House for three decades suggested that piecemeal earmarked funding for school districts—"$20 million here, or $30 million there"—worked in Evans's and Fumo's favor to whip up the votes they needed on other issues.

> The way that Dwight Evans used to control the Philly delegation, and also some other members, was to say, "I will be able to get us an extra thirty or $40 million for the School District of Philadelphia this year. But in exchange for that, I need you to vote for this, I need this to happen, and you can lay claim to the fact that you're getting an extra $40 million this year. And we're all going to hold a big press conference, and we're all going to beat our chests and we're going to say, 'Rah rah, look at what Philadelphia did.'" And I look at that and go, "Yeah, I'm glad you guys all fell for that, because really what you should have been doing was saying, 'No, Dwight. We want to change the funding formula, so that we get $40 million every year.'" But if you do that, as soon as you do that . . . the [rank-and-file] guy doesn't need you [the chair] for his funding, and so [as chair] you've got to figure out some other way to get them to vote for something. And so one of the ways to keep some of the members in line was to always keep them needing to ask for that extra funding, instead of building it into a formula.

As this representative explained, relying on earmarked funding was more advantageous to party leaders.

Piecemeal funding was political theater, garnering publicity for Philadelphia delegates year in and year out. Creating and implementing a fair funding formula that would hypothetically give Philadelphia "$40 million every year" would yield only one media blitz. But lack of a fair funding formula meant that Philadelphia would be allocated earmarked funding multiple times over the course of several years, creating more opportunities for media attention—the bread and butter for politicians. Earmarked funding had greater media currency and allowed Philadelphia delegates "to hold a big press conference, and . . . beat our chests and . . . say, 'Rah rah, look at what Philadelphia did.'"

Full implementation of a fair funding formula would have diminished the power of party leaders since Philadelphia delegates would no longer need party leaders to get them extra school funding. Piecemeal funding was a way to "keep some of the members in line . . . to always keep them needing to ask for that extra funding." Without the carrot and the stick of earmarked funding, party leaders had one less tool at their disposal to discipline rank-and-file members to vote a certain way on a myriad of issues. For party leaders, earmarked funding was a highly effective technique of control. There were potentially dire consequences for rank-and-file legislators who wanted to opt out of the game of earmarked funding: they risked falling out of favor with their party's leaders and/or losing their jobs as a result of negative or absent publicity. The system incentivized the continual use of earmarked funding and disincentivized a long-term solution to the problem of racial inequity in school funding.

## HOW THE SAUSAGE GETS MADE

To earmark funding for select school districts, legislators crafted idiosyncratic characteristics that only applied to those districts. In 2013, Senator Pat Browne, who occupied the position of Senate majority whip (2011–2014)—the fourth-highest-ranking leadership position in the Pennsylvania State Senate—was able to secure $8 million for the Allentown School District. According to reporting by *The Philadelphia Public School Notebook*, he accomplished this feat through inserting impenetrable and oddly specific language into the school code:

> (1) To qualify for the English language learner high incidence supplement, a school district's 2012–2013 market value/income aid ratio must be greater than seven thousand ten-thousandths (0.7000) and its English language learner concentration must be greater

than ten and eight-tenths percent (10.8 percent). (ii) the English language learner high incidence supplement shall be calculated for qualifying school districts as follows: (A) (i) For qualifying school districts with a 2011–2012 average daily membership greater than eighteen thousand five hundred (18,500), multiply the qualifying school district's 2011–2012 average daily membership by eight million dollars ($8,000,000). (ii) divide the product from subclause (i) by the sum of the 2011–2012 average daily membership for all qualifying school districts with a 2011–2012 average daily membership greater than eighteen thousand five hundred (18,500). (Socolar 2013)

How many school districts have a "2012–2013 market value/income aid ratio . . . greater than seven thousand ten-thousandth (0.7000) and [an] English language learner concentration . . . greater than ten and eight-tenths percent (10.8 percent)" (Socolar 2013)? *Only Allentown.*

The English Learner (EL) supplement that Allentown received was one of twelve different supplements created to disguise the allocation of earmarked funding to targeted districts. In addition to the EL supplement and a charter school supplement, there was: "a special growth supplement for districts adding enrollment, a small district supplement, a rural district supplement, a second class A county school district supplement, a third class county district supplement—and other such specialized categories" (Socolar 2013).

As further proof that districts were cherry-picked, "six of the 12 so-called formula changes, whose titles sound general, were written in such a way to benefit only one district each" (Socolar 2013)—none of which included Philadelphia. Philadelphia's fall from grace since the heyday of Rep. Evans and Senator Fumo meant that the district, "which has nearly half the charter students in the state and one-quarter of the English language learners, got none of these funds" (Socolar 2013). This was rubbing salt in the wound since that was also the year in which Philadelphia "was desperately begging the governor and legislature for additional state aid just to remain solvent" (Socolar 2013).

While some districts with high populations of English learners received funding, there was no correlation between the amount of earmarked funding allocated to a district and the number of English

### Table 1 · Earmarked Funding Lacks Rhyme or Reason

| School District | Student Population | Percent English Learners | Percent in Poverty | Earmarked Funding |
|---|---|---|---|---|
| Reading | ~ 18,400 | 18 percent | 87 percent | $1.5 million |
| Allentown | ~ 19,000 | 11 percent | 77 percent | $8 million |
| York | ~ 8,000 | 14 percent | 73 percent | $6.2 million |

Table 1 shows that higher amounts of earmarked funding allocated to a school district do not correlate with higher student population, higher percent of English learners, or higher percent of students living in poverty. *Source*: Education Law Center 2013a

learners or students in poverty in that district, as table 1 shows. Allentown received more than five times the amount of earmarked funding as Reading, even though Reading has a higher percentage of EL students and a higher percentage of students living in poverty (Education Law Center 2013a).

The Allentown School District has a student population that is majority-minority: 71 percent of its students are Latine, 15 percent Black, and only 9 percent white (Pennsylvania Department of Education, Data Collection Team 2013). The school district is the fourth biggest loser of hold harmful in the state; it is shortchanged $85 million, or over $4,000 per pupil. Clearly, Allentown needed the $8 million boost, and then some. But so did other school districts that didn't have a senator who was a high-ranking leader in the Pennsylvania Senate. These thinly disguised efforts to give money to select districts were not lost on observers. Sharon Ward, director of the Pennsylvania Budget and Policy Center, succinctly summarized her thoughts: "Legislators decided which particular districts were going to get money based on politics. Then they created those artificial supplements in order to drive money to those particular districts" (Socolar 2013). Senator Browne boasted about his district receiving the highest increase in basic education funding in the last decade, rather than stand in solidarity with other financially struggling districts; he secured earmarked money for his district through "artificial supplements," rather than fight for a systematic funding formula that would have given Allentown $85 million more *every year*.

Republican leaders were able to allocate earmarked funding through loopholes that circumvented regular channels—channels that were meant to provide checks and balances. Business casual Dan was incredulous about how decidedly undemocratic the process was. This loophole, he said, was "a huge problem. . . . It is indicative . . . of one of the most broken parts of the system because it removes any public input and it consolidates power with a handful of people, even if they are in the majority." He described the process of how earmarked funding is allocated to select districts:

> So every year, typically what happens with the budget is, there are omnibus bills—the code bills—there is a tax code bill; there is a school code bill; there's an administrative code bill. And they kind of take pieces of legislation that, you know, have moved or in some cases have just . . . the process is very much like "how the sausage gets made." situation. There are what I would call protocols, but there are no rules. There is this kind of unspoken thing where if you have a bill and it passes at least one chamber, then you can put it into the school code. . . . That sort of understanding and agreement gets changed for whoever is asking, right? So that may apply to a rank-and-file member, but for Senate Majority Leader Jake Corman, that does not apply. So if he wants something in the school code, he sends one of his people into that meeting where the school code is getting negotiated with a piece of language, and it goes in. And that's how it gets done [LIU: without having to pass any . . .] Nothing, nothing. And that's that. And so there are pieces that, just in this school code, that just passed, that were never, never even introduced as a bill.

Dan used the idiom "how the sausage gets made" to shed light on the process of earmarked funding—both are shrouded from public view, and both are unpleasant to witness. Not only was there a loose set of "protocols" that allowed a bill to be slipped into the school code if it passed just one chamber (whereas a normal bill is reviewed by both chambers and debated on), people in positions of leadership, like Senate Majority Leader Corman, could completely disregard these protocols. All he needed to do was send "one of his people into that meeting where the school code is getting negotiated with a piece of language, and it goes in." This abuse of power has enabled a system of school funding that is based on politics rather than student needs.

This loophole is why education policy organizations in Pennsylvania often pay close attention to what they refer to as "changes to the school code." Policy associates pore over the school code with a fine-toothed comb, taking note of what changes legislators are attempting to surreptitiously slip in under the radar. It wasn't until the interview with Dan that I understood that the seemingly innocuous phrase—"changes to the school code"—meant that state legislators were circumventing the normal process for policymaking.

For comparison's sake, for HB 961—the 100 percent full and fair funding bill supported by POWER and introduced by Representative Rabb—to be passed into law, it would have to undergo eight steps:

1. The birth of an idea;
2. The development of a written bill with a number assigned to it;
3. Scrutiny by a relevant standing committee;
4. Peer review in majority and minority caucuses;
5. Vote on the House floor;
6. Appraisal by the Senate;
7. Signed into law by the governor;
8. The bill is repackaged as a law and given a new number and title. (Office of the Chief Clerk n.d.)

About "75 percent of the bills received in the Standing Committee are never considered because they are identified as irrelevant, too similar to other bills, poor policy, too narrow in focus, or a distraction from more vital issues" (Office of the Chief Clerk n.d.). Although Representative Rabb's HB 961 had sixty-three cosponsors, it has been stuck in the second step of this process because Chairperson Sonney of the Education Committee was unwilling to give the bill a hearing. While this has been the fate of HB 961, in sharp contrast, "there are pieces that just in this [2019] school code that just passed that were never, never even introduced as a bill," as Dan stated. Republican leadership steamrolled over all the intermediary steps that are usually required for a bill to become law. Dan soberly noted that voting "no" was "entirely symbolic" since "Republicans control both chambers and really don't necessarily have to involve Democrats to get votes to pass." School funding is beholden to Republican leaders who have used their power to maintain the racial school funding status quo.

As Dan stated, earmarked funding in Pennsylvania is an example of "one of the most broken parts of the system." Party leaders used their power and position to create artificial supplements that often only applied to their own select districts and then slipped those artificial supplements into the school code, circumventing the democratic aspects of lawmaking. With a foolproof majority, there was little to stand in their way.

## THE SHELL GAME OF EARMARKED FUNDING

In 2014, after press scrutiny of earmarked funds, legislative leaders played an elaborate shell game to move funds from one budgetary line item to another. During that year, "the state drastically cut earmarked funding to $3.95 million and assigned it to a new budgetary line item called the Educational Access Program, which the state never defined" (Hawkes 2018). Then, between 2015 and 2017, the Educational Access Program line item ballooned from $6 million to $23.15 million, suggesting that earmarked funds had been moved to elude detection (Hawkes 2018).

Rep. Hickernell, a Republican from Lancaster County, was fed up with the lack of transparency and a political process that overlooked the needs of one of his school districts. Hickernell's legislative district included the beleaguered Columbia Borough School District that was a $2.8 million "loser" because of hold harmful. Sixty-six percent of Columbia students were eligible for free or reduced lunch and 50 percent of them were students of color (Education Law Center 2013a). During the 2017–2018 legislative session, Rep. Hickernell introduced legislation (HB 1744) to "prohibit special funding to select school districts" (Hickernell 2019). Fifty representatives signed onto his bill.

Legislative leaders took notice and zeroed out the Educational Access Program line item, only to use Ready-to-Learn grants to continue to funnel earmarked money to cherry-picked districts. During 2018–2019, the line item for Ready-to-Learn grants grew by $18 million to a total of $268 million (Hawkes 2018). While $250 million was dedicated to the routine administration of Ready-to-Learn grants (which districts could apply for), $18 million was selectively reserved for three districts. On February 13, 2019, Rep. Hickernell reintroduced legislation (now HB 976) to prohibit earmarked funding, indicating the problem had not gone away.

Hickernell's 2019 bill specifically cited the Erie School District as an example of a district that received earmarked funding. Referring to Erie, Hickernell's 2019 bill stated that "language was included in the Fiscal Code to make this $14 Million part of the District's base Basic Education Funding (BEF) allocation which they would get each year" (Hickernell 2019). Erie's earmarked funding was slipped into the administrative codes using the following hyper-specific language:

> (c) Educational access program funding.—The amount of educational access program funding received in the 2017–2018 fiscal year by a school district identified for financial watch status under section 694-A of the Public School Code of 1949, during the 2016–2017 school year shall be deemed to be a part of the school district's allocation amount under section 2502.53(b)(1) of the Public School Code of 1949 for the 2017–2018 school year and each school year thereafter. (Pennsylvania General Assembly 2017)

The above language goes to great pains to obfuscate what can be plainly stated: *Erie School District will be allocated an extra $14 million every year, from now on.* According to a staffer, earmarked funding is a game where "analysts like me who're getting a draft of this have to go and say, 'What school district is this?'"

Unlike how most earmarked funding was allocated—that is, through high-ranking legislative leaders advocating for their districts—Erie's additional $14 million was achieved through the advocacy of its superintendent. When I spoke to people who were familiar with the Erie deal, I asked how the school district was able to secure the additional funds, since the district was not represented by state Republican leaders. They pointed to how the superintendent, Jay Badams, was a vocal advocate for his district and became "a fixture in the capital for a while." One staffer recalled that Superintendent

Badams made several different trips to Harrisburg and even hired a lobbyist. Another remembers him bringing parents and "they would have these big rallies" and he would "get all red in the face and get very emotional." Like Allentown School District, there is no doubt that Erie needed the money. Before they were awarded the extra $14 million, the district, which serves 36 percent Black students and 14 percent Latine students (Pennsylvania Department of Education, Data Collection Team 2013), was shorted $12 million of its fair share. And yet a district's ability to be equitably funded should neither depend on how "red in the face" its superintendent can get, nor its ability to make seven separate ten-hour trips to Harrisburg. Is that what it takes to compel state legislators to do something? Students in underfunded districts deserve better.

The shell game of earmarked funding was so effective that most legislators were unaware of the allocations until an announcement was made in the media. *LNP* reported in 2018 that "Even rank-and-file lawmakers complain they're in the dark" (Hawkes 2018). Senator Scott Martin, a first-term Republican from Lancaster, stated, "We don't necessarily know what any of this is until all of a sudden there's a press release hailing whoever for securing the money" (Hawkes 2018). Perplexed by such press releases, he asked, "How does this work? Explain this to me. I thought the legislature had to approve spending" (Hawkes 2018). While the legislature was responsible for approving spending, rank-and-file legislators were so disoriented by the language and constant shuffling of money from one line item to another, they often did not understand what they were approving until it was too late. Zeroing out one line item, only to divert money to another line item, gave the *appearance* that earmarked funding had ended, but allowed Republican leaders to continue to exploit their power and position for their districts' financial gain.

## EARMARKED FUNDING STIFLES SOLIDARITY

Though earmarked funding primarily benefited districts with significant populations of Black and Brown children, it has come at a great cost to the very same students it purports to benefit. The celebration of earmarked funding by legislators sends the message that these districts and these children should settle for less; they should accommodate. In the grand scheme of things, earmarked funding was a drop in the bucket. In 2013, $30 million of earmarked funding was allocated out of a total state education budget of $6 billion, or 0.5 percent. But this comparatively small amount of money has been exploited by state legislators to congratulate themselves and to appear to be school funding advocates in the public eye, while refusing to make any substantial changes.

The Allentown School District and its state legislators illustrate this point. Even after *LNP*'s reporting of earmarked funds in 2013, Senator Browne and Representatives Schlossberg and Schweyer, all legislators of the Allentown School District, immediately took credit for their "major win" in 2018 and gloated about it in a press release. Rep. Schlossberg crowed: "It goes without saying that this is a major win for Allentown students, teachers and taxpayers. The additional funding we supported will help ensure that our children can get the kind of high quality education they deserve, and there is nothing more important to the success of our community" (Moyer and Andrews 2018). Similarly, Senator Browne stated:

> It is critical that the state provides the necessary resources to school districts, especially those in challenged areas like Allentown, to ensure all Pennsylvania students have access to a quality education. I am pleased to have worked with my colleagues in the House, Representatives Schlossberg and Schweyer, to provide this vital funding. (Moyer and Andrews 2018)

Though Browne's statement was more tempered, like Schlossberg, he took credit for the "vital funding" that Allentown received and asserted the importance of the state's obligation to provide "the necessary resources to school districts, especially those in challenged areas like Allentown, to ensure all Pennsylvania students have access to a quality education" (Moyer and Andrews 2018). Yet these statements lack sincerity considering Senator Browne's track record.

Time after time, Senator Browne occupied roles that could have made major advances, but he punted on each and every opportunity to enact a racially equitable system of school funding. Browne not only served as cochair of the 2014 BEF Commission (alongside Mike Vereb), but he also served as majority whip (2010–2014) and majority chair of the Appropriations Committee (2014–2022)—positions he could have leveraged to enact substantive change. According to a policy analyst who commented on Browne's powerful role as chair of the Senate Appropriations Committee:

> [Senator Browne] not only has a seat at the budget table, he picks where the table is. He has a lot of power and influence. . . . He can control the spending bill in the Senate; he can hold it up; he controls which amendments go into it. . . . And just being in the majority, they control the agenda in which bills run.

Senator Browne's seeming-advocacy of public education, expressed in the 2018 press release, rings hollow when one considers his failure to use his substantial "power and influence" to create the kind of change that majority-minority districts "in challenged areas like Allentown" desperately needed (Moyer and Andrews 2018).

At the time of Browne's press release in 2018, the fair funding formula already existed for two years. Instead of pushing the legislature to drive all the money through the formula, which would have given Allentown an extra $85 million every year and obviated the need for earmarked funding, Browne was content with taking credit for the "vital" $10 million he secured. By advocating for a small accommodation of earmarked funding for Allentown, he was undermining efforts to, in his own words, "ensure all Pennsylvania students have access to a quality education" (Moyer and Andrews 2018). Senator Browne's political maneuvering facilitated earmarked funds for Allentown, but the process excluded other equally needy or needier districts. Browne's influence in maintaining the policy of hold harmful and to earmark funds for Allentown necessarily ensured that not all Pennsylvania children would have access to a quality education.

Senator Browne is depicted as an antagonist in this story, and yet by many accounts, he is well respected for his commitment to bipartisanship, which led to the 2016 adoption of a fair funding formula. Several Democrats described him as someone who is reasonable to work with. One Democratic representative heralded Senator Browne as a "great guy" "who I have a lot of respect for." A person working within a campaign for fair funding, described Browne as "our only Republican ally. . . . He's our guy. And actually, he's our only Republican." It's reasonable to infer that a different senator in the same leadership position would not have achieved as much as Senator Browne did. Through compromise and accommodation, he managed to get Allentown an extra $10 million. But what did this actually accomplish for Black and Brown children in Pennsylvania? And at what cost? Rewarding some districts with earmarked funds purchases the silence of "winner" districts and hampers solidarity building among all majority-Black-and-Brown districts; it curtails the urgency to collectively fight for a long-term solution to inequitable funding. *Be satisfied with what you get* is the message of earmarked funding.

If state legislators obstructed systemic change through use of earmarked school funding, then colorblind advocacy was the corollary of how campaigns prevented change. Some coalitions espoused change but were in the business of preserving the racial school funding status quo. The remaining chapters foreground coalitional politics and how organizers and advocates interacted with state legislators. I take a close look at campaigns that seem similar from the outside but have very different orientations toward race and school funding. Chapter 4 provides historical context for understanding recent campaigns for school funding, demonstrating that the colorblind advocacy we see today didn't appear out of thin air; rather, it was informed by the highly contentious battles that Superintendent David Hornbeck had with state legislators in the late 1990s. His race-confrontational approach in demanding funding for Philly schools rankled state legislators and facilitated the state takeover of the district. Many of today's school funding advocates have visceral memories of these highly public losses and associate it with the danger of taking a race-conscious approach toward advocacy. Meanwhile, some of the most substantial school funding wins were achieved through a colorblind approach. These were the lessons learned by some of today's school funding advocates and provide an important context for understanding the dynamics of today's school funding coalitions.

## CHAPTER FOUR

# Race-Conscious Losses and Colorblind Wins during the Hornbeck and Rendell Eras

The landscape of school funding advocacy in Pennsylvania involves people of different political stripes. Several organizations committed to racially equitable school funding espouse a form of "progressive" politics—that is, they are considerably left of center-left, or left of Biden for a more concrete reference point. These organizations are informed by the works of Cheryl Harris, Monique Morris, and Bryan Stevenson; they work to dismantle the school-to-prison pipeline; they celebrate the victories of local progressive politicians like Helen Gym and Kendra Brooks; they advocate for Philadelphia students; they have spoken publicly and forcefully against racial injustices in education; and they believe that colorblindness is another form of racism. So I couldn't understand why some of these same organizations were part of a school funding coalition that practiced colorblindness and sidelined evidence of racial bias in school funding. This chapter provides a historical context for understanding how the failure of past race-explicit approaches shaped the colorblind strategies of contemporary school funding campaigns. The very real losses that were suffered by taking a race-conscious approach have served as a cautionary tale to advocates today.

Relatedly, the "wins" that were attained through colorblind strategies have bolstered the salience of that approach. "When winning is losing" is a phrase and concept, developed by Savannah Shange, that critiques how progressive reforms and "wins" "domesticate our freedom dreams within the realm of what's possible, rather than what's necessary" (Shange 2019:18). She argues that progressive reforms may "enact the best-case scenario for surviving late liberalism" (Shange 2019:18), but progressivism is still another formulation of the afterlife of slavery. Through this lens, the more immediate "wins" that politicians and advocates fought for can be viewed as "losses" because they served to obscure the very real racial inequities in school funding, and in doing so, maintained these inequalities.

In the context of Pennsylvania politics, these "wins" were consequential and cause for celebration. Achieving the development of a funding formula and a funding target were no small feats. And yet, these achievements were either short-lived, undone by the next administration, or they were nominal, making a small impact on actual schooling conditions. When "winning" relies on promoting colorblind logics, it comes at a considerable cost because it conceals deeply embedded structures of racism and white privilege.

## LESSONS LEARNED FROM SUPERINTENDENT HORNBECK'S RACE-CONFRONTATIONAL APPROACH

From 1994 to 2000, David Hornbeck served as superintendent of Philadelphia schools. During this time, the district faced a major financial crisis, due in large part to the policy of hold harmful that did not provide increased funding commensurate with the district's growing student enrollment. Between 1990 and 1991 and 1997 and 1998 (at the height of the district's financial crisis), Philadelphia's student population had grown significantly, from 191,000 students to its peak of 213,000 students. However, because state funding remained stagnant, per-pupil funding decreased significantly during that time. Pennsylvania's share of state aid had plummeted from a high of nearly 50 percent in 1971–1972 to a low of 36 percent by 1995–1996. As a result, the School District of Philadelphia was on the brink of financial ruin during Hornbeck's tenure as superintendent.

Hornbeck believed that the district's financial crisis was related to the racial background of its students. In 1997–1998, the school district was made up of 64 percent Black students; 19 percent white students; 12 percent Latine students; and 5 percent Asian students. Hornbeck is famously remembered for using the word *apartheid* to refer to Pennsylvania's system of education; he also blasted the state's school funding structure as racist and pushed lawmakers to provide the necessary funding to Philadelphia schools (Mezzacappa 2017).

In 1998, staring down the barrel of an $85 million shortfall, Superintendent Hornbeck sought to underscore the severity of the school funding problem and the state's neglect (Mezzacappa 2017). He was one of the people who conceived of the federal lawsuit *Powell v. Ridge* (1998), alleging that Pennsylvania's school funding formula "had a disparate negative impact on minority students and thus violated the Civil Rights Act of 1964" (Public Interest Law Center n.d.). Furthermore, Hornbeck created a standoff between Philadelphia and the state legislature, intending to force lawmakers to reckon with their responsibility to properly fund Philly schools.

The confrontation began after his pleas for more funding were ignored. Governor Ridge's spokesperson commented: "Hornbeck has not successfully focused on the first step of this equation, which is how Philadelphia's schools are spending the money they have now" (Tabor 1996). Hornbeck is white, but this comment notably casts aspersions on how "Philadelphia's schools"—majority-Black—spend their money. The racialized nature of these comments was not lost on Hornbeck who recalled how state lawmakers analogized giving money to Philadelphia as "sending money down the rat hole—and they really did use that kind of language on a routine basis" (Sanchez 2013). In a variation of the term, several people told me that lawmakers frequently talked about giving money to Philadelphia schools as putting money into a "black hole." Rather than take aim at the chronic underfunding of schools, comments from the governor's office drew on a long history of stereotyping Black people as spendthrifts to question their ability to self-govern.

Despite the lack of additional funding from the state, Hornbeck refused to balance the budget, which would have required him to significantly cut personnel and programs (Mezzacappa 2017). Instead, Philadelphia's Board of Education was prepared to pass a budget with an $85 million shortfall—an outcome that would have forced the schools to close in March when the money ran out (Mezzacappa 2017). This dramatic showdown was meant to "viscerally demonstrate the [state] funding formula's inadequacy" (Backer 2017).

Instead of forcing the hand of state lawmakers, Hornbeck's strategy backfired and opened the door to the state takeover of Philadelphia schools (Mezzacappa 2017). Nationally, state takeovers of urban school districts curtailed Black political power in cities across America in the late 1980s (Morel 2018). Pennsylvania was following in these footsteps. Act 46—a bipartisan deal between a Democratic-controlled state legislature and Republican Governor Ridge—was passed in 1999, allowing the state to take over school districts in "financial or academic distress" (Backer 2017). An *Inquirer* article opined: "Indeed, one thing that helped sell the state-takeover scenario was a rising tide of anti-Hornbeck sentiment in Harrisburg—where many upstate legislators already view Philadelphia as a wasteful money pit" (Moran 1998). Invoking Act 46 meant that the state could take power away from a locally controlled board by installing its own state-appointed members. This was a classic case of the fox guarding the henhouse. By maintaining a policy of hold harmful that failed to properly fund school districts, the governor and state legislature created the twin problems of financial and academic distress. Yet they gave themselves governance power over these "failing" districts. In another blow to Philadelphia, the legislation also curtailed the power of the teachers' union by limiting their collective bargaining and ability to strike (Backer 2017).

Dwight Evans, one of the chief architects of Act 46, was at the time a state legislator representing Philadelphia, and is now a member of the US House of Representatives. He occupied a powerful position as chair of the Pennsylvania House Appropriations Committee. In assessing Representative Evans's role in the underfunding of Philadelphia schools, David Backer (2017) stated:

> When Evans introduced Act 46, he had a choice of strategies: he could have supported the demand to properly fund the school district, drawing from the political and legal tradition of the civil rights movement to help the plaintiffs in *Powell v. Ridge*. Instead, he paved the way for an undemocratic takeover of city schools.

Representative Evans, who is Black, attended Philadelphia schools and had become frustrated with the state of public education. He was one of the founders of the Black Alliance for Educational Options, a pro-voucher organization established in 2000. Charter school growth in Philadelphia was the result of weak oversight of the state's charter school law that was passed in 1997, and the result of Act 46, which initiated the state takeover of the Philadelphia school district in 2001.[1] From 1997 until 2016, a total of ninety-seven charter schools were approved in Philadelphia. In 2018–2019, the School District of Philadelphia sent 28 percent of its $3.5 billion budget to charter schools, or $968 million—another major factor for the school district's financial woes. Dwight Evans also vocally opposed David Hornbeck.

With the writing on the wall, Hornbeck resigned from the superintendency in June 2000, after "years of rancorous and often fruitless battles with state lawmakers" (Johnston 2000). In a move that portended the power shift and Hornbeck's resignation, Mayor Street and his school board president, Pedro Ramos, negotiated a deal with the state legislature that gave the district enough money to stay open until the end of the 2000–2001 academic year, on the condition that the district would cut $30 million from its 2001–2002 budget (Johnston 2000). After the deal was made, Representative Evans underscored his lack of confidence in Hornbeck, stating: "Mr. Hornbeck did not have the ability to negotiate with the major players—the state legislature and the governor. This is what Mayor Street and Mr. Ramos are able to do" (Johnston 2000).

Perhaps one of the primary lessons that Hornbeck learned during his time as superintendent was that expressing his unvarnished opinion of Pennsylvania's racist school-funding structure ultimately undermined his goal. I spoke with Paul Socolar, a longtime journalist and founder of *The Philadelphia Public School Notebook*, about the Hornbeck era. His slender frame and mild manner belie the fact that he is considered a giant in matters of Philadelphia education. Well known for his encyclopedic knowledge of Philadelphia school issues, the chair of the board for *The Notebook* once said, "Paul has been almost a singular force in advancing the discussion of public issues in Philadelphia" (Langland 2015).

Socolar cited Hornbeck's approach with the state legislature as a "cautionary tale" of how some tactics can "shut down any work on racial justice." In 1999, Hornbeck gave a speech in which he referenced a disturbing front-page photograph in the *New York Times* of a young man with his hands cut off during the war in Sierra Leone. Hornbeck stated that it was a "'good metaphor' for the treatment of poor children in the United States" (Mezzacappa 1999). Elsewhere in the speech, he railed against state legislators and a "system that results in children of color, nonnative English speakers, disabled kids and poor children in general having larger classes and no access to prekindergarten programs, lousy libraries and fewer textbooks, and less access to technology" (Mezzacappa 1999).

To say that this speech was poorly received by state leaders would be an understatement. Governor Ridge's spokesperson referred to Hornbeck's remarks as "off the wall" and said that Hornbeck's "number one goal is moral superiority over the rest of us" (Mezzacappa 1999). Ridge and state lawmakers cited Hornbeck's "confrontational rhetoric and lawsuits seeking more funds from the state as a barrier to negotiating a solution to the fiscal crisis. . . . They [were] particularly offended by his clear implication that racism underl[ay] that decision" (Mezzacappa 1999). Applying these lessons from the past to the current struggle for additional funding, Socolar said:

> [Hornbeck's] communication around what was going on in Philadelphia was very . . . morally righteous I guess. . . . And I have to say that that probably was not helpful in terms of efforts to move the school funding cause forward in Harrisburg. He was ridiculed and dismissed as, you know, just a moralistic elitist.

Hornbeck's incendiary comparison and overall uncompromising style came off as "morally righteous" to some, and likely as a white savior to others. It further antagonized the already frayed relationship between Philadelphia and Harrisburg lawmakers. Just as Hornbeck was "ridiculed and dismissed," these events likely forced today's school funding advocates to think twice about whether a race-conscious approach would also be ridiculed and dismissed.

Understandably, many school funding advocates who vividly remember Hornbeck's time as superintendent see his failed negotiations with the state legislature, the defeat of *Powell v. Ridge* in federal court, and the backlash of the state takeover as a "cautionary tale" of what not to do. As Camika Royal (2022:87) remarked: "Hornbeck had a racial analysis of schooling in Philadelphia, but he lacked a concomitant strategy for mitigating the racism embedded in the school funding nexus so Philly schools could get what they needed." Given the anti-Philadelphia impulse in the state legislature, Hornbeck's style—one which forced lawmakers to confront their obligation to a majority-Black school district—ultimately backfired, creating adversaries on both sides of the aisle, including from state lawmakers who represented Philadelphia, like Rep. Evans. A lesson learned from his time as superintendent was that taking a race-confrontational approach not only failed to secure more funding for Philadelphia, but also resulted in a bipartisan state takeover of the district and the acceleration of charter schools. This history informed later approaches to school funding advocacy and is remembered as an example of how some approaches can "shut down any work on racial justice."

## "ANTI-PHILADELPHIA BIAS"

The state legislature's anti-Philadelphia sentiments experienced by Hornbeck during his superintendency have deep roots and are related to a narrative of scarcity that encourages racist stereotypes about people of color. Keeanga-Yamahtta Taylor has observed the following:

> When it comes to schools, housing, food, and other basic necessities, politicians always complain about deficits and the need to curb spending and cut budgets. The scarcity is manufactured, but the competition over these resources is real. People who are forced to fight over basic necessities are often willing to believe the worst about other[s] to justify why they should have something while others should not. (Taylor 2016:212)

According to several Pennsylvania state legislators and staff, the fight over basic necessities is often expressed in "anti-urban," "anti-Philadelphia" (read: anti-Black) attitudes and the impression that Philadelphia, a majority-Black city, receives more than it should.

In a conversation I had with a Democratic state representative from Philadelphia, he explained why getting more school funding for Philadelphia, among other issues, was an intractable problem in Harrisburg:

*Legislator:* Part of the problem is that there is a very strong . . . I'll be nice . . . anti-urban bias, that's an anti-Philadelphia bias, and many people would say, "Oh, the state tilts and all the money goes into Philadelphia." Well, that's not true at all.

*Liu:* So you had said it's an anti-urban, but especially anti-Philadelphia [bias]. What are the reasons for that?

*Legislator:* Well because we suck all the money out of the state.

*Liu:* That's the thinking?

*Legislator:* No, I'm just saying that's a perception, that we get all the money. That's not true. For example, you talk about school subsidies. We get a school subsidy. But I understand the Philadelphia school district is far larger than most of the districts in this state, and we're the largest district in the state, but the numbers are disproportionate. So when you see the amount of money that the state gives to Philadelphia, it's like, "Oh, they're getting too much money." But that's reflected in the number of students we have.

In fact, Philadelphia was not only the largest school district in Pennsylvania, but it also educates 12 percent of all public school students in the entire state. But because of its size, legislators had the impression that Philadelphia received "too much money." This state representative suggested that calling it an "anti-urban," "anti-Philadelphia" bias was a "nice" way of putting it. In a city and school district with a significant Black population (42 percent in the city and 52 percent in the school district in 2021), this was a diplomatic spin on the anti-Black culture that pervades in the state legislature.

Anti-Blackness and anti–big city were two sides of the same coin, according to a Democratic staffer I spoke with. "One strand," he said, "is simple . . . that people don't understand the number, the size. And then the other pieces, just very simply, I think xenophobia, racism." He continued to say, "whatever side of the coin you want to focus on"—that is, whether you choose to be "nice" by chalking it up to legislators who don't understand the size of Philadelphia, or you focus on the anti-Black subtext of geography and size—these sentiments were "incredibly real, incredibly out-front, incredibly blatant all the time, every day," said the staffer. To cite an example, he said that in a committee meeting, "one of the representatives from Philly will start saying something. And some, you know, some House members, you know, from the middle of the state will say . . . 'Why don't we just blow it up?'"

Violent responses to the threat of a decline in white hegemony is disturbing, though unsurprising given the January 6th attack on the US Capitol by a disgruntled white mob of Trump supporters in 2021. It reminds us of the American impulse to use force to maintain white supremacy when it is in jeopardy. In the immediate days after the Capitol riots, historians and public scholars reflected on other instances when angry white mobs sought to violently upend the results of free and fair elections that strengthened multiracial democracy (Serwer 2021; Wasow 2021). Contrary to President-elect Biden's characterization of the Capitol attacks as "un-American," they argued that its resonance was, in fact, very American, and very much in keeping with the nation's past. As this Democratic staffer said himself, the anti-Philadelphia bias is "not just about Pennsylvania and Philadelphia, but it's about our country."

Many Pennsylvania state legislators fear that Philadelphia represents a bellwether for where the state and country are heading. These fears were realized in the 2020 presidential election when Philadelphia helped to deliver a decisive repudiation of Trump's racist policies. The antagonism against Philadelphia, represented viscerally by the question—"Why don't we just blow it up?"—should be interpreted and understood within this long national history of racial violence in response to attempts to weaken white supremacy.

Moreover, to state legislators, Philadelphia was emblematic of a kind of Blackness that was unruly, excessive, and ungovernable. When another state legislator told me that the contempt for Philadelphia had to do with the perception that it received "special treatment," I asked why the city is so often seen that way. He responded:

> Look, I don't want to cast aspersions on my colleagues, but I've heard it speculated—I'll say, that way I'm not the one making an accusation—I've heard it speculated that it has to do, in large part with the color of those kids' skin. . . . And, you know, in Pittsburgh, there are white kids and kids of color, but they're midwestern Black kids in Pittsburgh. They aren't, you know, hardcore East Coast . . . Philly gang, Black, you know, Muslim kids.

This state legislator characterized his colleagues as making a distinction between "Black kids in Pittsburgh" and Black kids from Philly who were presumably affiliated with "gang[s]" and "Muslim." Within this list of purported offenses—"hardcore," "gang," "Muslim"—it is *Muslim* that initially stands out as inconsistent with the others. *Muslim* only coheres with the rest of the list if we understand the list to be characteristics that are seen as antithetical to the "heartland"—that is, white, midwestern, Christian values. "Black kids in Pittsburgh" were seen as tenuously assimilable in the liberal project of citizenship; Black kids from Philly were not.

While these racist discourses feel incredibly contemporary, they emerge from discursive fields and classificatory logics that are incredibly old—as old as the idea of "the West" itself—dating back to the Renaissance period. During the Renaissance and successively nurtured by different waves of colonialism, the Enlightenment, and slavery in the Americas (Trouillot 2003:19), the "savage slot" was constructed as a foil that enabled Eurocentric ideas of "the West" to flourish. This geography of imagination was marked by coterminous, yet Janus-faced dichotomies: the West–the Rest; Order–Savage; State–Utopia; The Observer–The Other; Culture–Nature; History–Stories; Here–Elsewhere (Trouillot 2003:23), and I would add, Christian–Muslim, given how "Christendom became Europe, [and] Europe itself became Christian" with the conquest of the Muslim kingdom of Granada in 1492 (Trouillot 2003:20). *Islam* was constructed as dichotomous to notions of "the West," and put in service of colonial conquests in the New World and the slave trade, making it central to early US racial formation (Rana 2007). These "old" (but still very much existent) geographies of imagination have been localized in the way state legislators imagine children and youth in Pennsylvania.

Through their discourse of Black youth in Pennsylvania, state legislators reanimate the dichotomies of Order–Savage and the West–the Rest. In this case, "the West" is mapped onto a small "w"—"the west" of western PA—but still assigned a positive valence, giving "midwestern Black kids in Pittsburgh" a quality of "goodness." In other words, "Black kids in Pittsburgh" stem from the same lineage as the trope of the "noble savage." The "noble savage" of Pittsburgh is imagined to be assimilable and could, or at least *should* eventually become like "us." But as Michel-Rolph Trouillot (2003:23) notes: "The Savage can be noble, wise, barbaric, victim or aggressor, depending on the debate and on the aims of the interlocutors. The space within the slot is not static, and its changing contents are not pre-determined by its structural position. Regional and temporal variants of the Savage abound." Given the debate on school funding and with the aim of illustrating the undeservedness of Philadelphia youth, if Pittsburgh Black children were seen as the "noble savage," then Black children in Philadelphia were constructed as the "barbaric savage"—that is, "hardcore," "gang," and "Muslim"—and ultimately undeserving of state resources.

The Pittsburgh-Philly dynamic is analogous to broader notions of "good" and "bad" that hinge on racial demographics. In the same way that notions of a "good school" often rely on higher percentages of white students, Pittsburgh is viewed by state legislators as a "good" city with "good" Black kids because it is a whiter city (67 percent white) and school district (32 percent) than Philadelphia (36 percent white residents; 14 percent white students). The Pittsburgh School District also happens to be one of the few cities that receives $78 million *more than* the amount calculated by the fair funding formula.

"Anti-Philadelphia" bias circulates rampantly in the state capitol and provides an explanation for why state legislators are so unwilling to create school funding policies that would benefit Philadelphia. This bias is fed by a myth of scarcity, which positions Philadelphia as an undeserving competitor in state resources and creates a racial wedge between underfunded majority-white and majority-minority school districts that have more in common than they think. White rural districts have so far been willing to forgo systemic change, instead settling for not being at the bottom of the school-funding hierarchy.

## WHITE SOLIDARITY

Like many cases in history, potential class solidarity among underfunded school districts has been undermined by white privilege and white solidarity, even though majority-white affluent school districts have played a major role in the inequities experienced by majority-white underfunded districts. The dynamic in which white privilege mitigates class tensions has resonances with the past. Institutional slavery in the US created a social dynamic in which "whites who were small farmers and those who were big planters had nothing in common except that they were not slaves, and that eased the potential tensions between them" (Taylor 2016:209). Continuing into the Jim Crow era, "white workers perceived they had more in common with the bourgeoisie than with fellow workers who were Black" (Harris 1993:1741). Indeed, there were benefits to claiming whiteness over standing in solidarity with Black workers: white worker wages were higher, and they enjoyed an elevated status in public life, gaining access to better-funded public facilities.

Schools played an important role in the construction and claiming of whiteness since "White schoolhouses were the best in the community, and conspicuously placed, and they cost anywhere from twice to ten times as much per capita as the colored schools" (Du Bois 1998:701). Poor and working-class whites were comforted by the fact that their children could attend schools that were more well-funded than segregated Black schools. In the United States' so-called War on Drugs, politicians passed increasingly harsher drug laws that had a disproportionately negative impact on Black people to "appeal to poor and working-class whites who, once again, proved they were willing to forego economic and structural reform in exchange for an apparent effort to put blacks back 'in their place'" (Alexander 2012:191).

The dynamics of white solidarity, seen throughout history, help us understand the racial antagonisms in Pennsylvania school funding. In a one-two punch, Pennsylvania state legislators fostered white solidarity by first invisibilizing the role of majority-white affluent school districts in wealth hoarding, and then preserving hold harmful to give underfunded majority-white districts a comparative advantage over underfunded majority-minority school districts. Take for example, the wealth hoarding of affluent majority-white districts like Radnor. In 2019–2020, Radnor had a 71 percent white share, and its local taxing capacity alone allowed it to raise about $21,900 per child—*double* the state average local per-pupil revenue of $10,700. Districts like Radnor are unbothered by the state's low contribution to school funding because of its high local wealth.

But instead of addressing this wealth hoarding and overreliance on local taxing capacity, Republican state legislators zeroed in on preserving hold harmful to mitigate the class tensions that might otherwise exist between majority-white working-class rural districts and majority-white affluent suburban districts. Take for example, a comparison between the Albert Gallatin School District and the School District of Philadelphia. Hovering at 35 percent, Albert Gallatin has a poverty rate like that of Philadelphia (36 percent). But this is where the similarities end. In 2019–2020, Albert Gallatin had a white student population of 92 percent, compared to Philadelphia's white share of 14 percent; Albert Gallatin's local contribution to total revenue was 25 percent, compared to Philadelphia's much higher local contribution of 40 percent; the state's contribution to Albert Gallatin's total revenue was a staggering 70 percent, compared to Philadelphia's much lower state share of 43 percent; finally and importantly, because of the preservation of hold harmful, Albert Gallatin received $2,400 *more* per pupil than its fair funding formula calculation, whereas Philadelphia received about $2,000 *less* per pupil than the formula calculation.

Radnor's role in wealth hoarding and Albert Gallatin's potential solidarity with Philadelphia is attenuated by the policy of hold harmful that gives Gallatin $2,400 more per pupil than it would otherwise receive. State Republicans' objection against raising new taxes that would adequately fund school districts with weak local taxing capacities has forced underfunded majority-white rural districts to fight against underfunded majority-minority urban schools for a share of state aid that has shrunk significantly since the 1980s. It is precisely this zero-sum game that has entrenched antagonisms between these districts— districts that would have more to gain if they worked together. Poor and working-class white Pennsylvania districts have been willing to forgo systemic changes that would improve their current conditions, so long as they hold a comparative advantage over majority-minority school districts.

## THE PENNSYLVANIA SCHOOL FUNDING CAMPAIGN'S COLORBLIND "WIN" (2005–2014)

After resigning from the superintendency, Hornbeck sought to continue his commitment to ensuring that poor majority-minority school districts like Philadelphia got their fair share of funding through the work of Good Schools PA. Good Schools, founded in 2001 by a group of religious and educational leaders including Hornbeck, provided an organizing and grassroots dimension to school funding advocacy. As a graduate of Union Theological Seminary and as someone who aspired to become a minister, Hornbeck's theory of change was shaped by a faith tradition of activism. Good Schools PA, along with the Education Law Center-PA (ELC) and Education Policy and Leadership Center (EPLC), launched the Pennsylvania School Funding Campaign (PSFC) in 2005.

From the beginning, PSFC took a decidedly statewide perspective on the problem of school funding, conveying that school funding is "not an urban problem, a rural problem, or any single school district's problem. It's the problem, and responsibility, of all citizens in the state, whether they live in the state's richest or poorest school district" (Rhodes 2004). Given the anti-Philadelphia impulse in Harrisburg that Hornbeck experienced firsthand, PSFC's framing of school funding as a *statewide* problem downplayed the role of Philadelphia, and by extension, the role of structural racism in school funding, which better appealed to the sensibilities of state lawmakers.

The campaign sought to dispel the common belief that school funding inequities were only the result of local disparities, as this campaign member explained:

> I would be talking to school districts; they almost always thought the problem in funding their schools was what they were doing in their district and rarely thought about, "Hey, maybe the problem is in Harrisburg." And that's what we tried to do. To make it clear that what was happening was the state was increasing its reliance on local funding, decreasing the state share of the burden, and that this was a Harrisburg problem.

PSFC raised awareness of how "maybe the problem is in Harrisburg." It educated the public on how the distribution of *state* aid was inequitable and built support around lobbying for change through *state* channels—a strategy that would be repeated in subsequent coalitions. As the first coalition for school funding in Pennsylvania, PSFC served as a model for future campaigns and coalitions, and convened organizations and people who would be decades-long stalwarts of school funding.

EPLC, one of the three organizations that launched PSFC, was led by Ron Cowell, a white former state representative of Pennsylvania. EPLC aimed to "encourage and support the development and implementation of effective state-level education policies" (Education Policy and Leadership Center n.d.). Its signature program, the Education Policy Fellowship Program, cultivated educational leaders from various sectors, including education, government, nonprofit, and business. Among other things, the program developed participants' knowledge of school funding issues so they could more effectively press for change in their respective leadership positions. Cowell's experience as a twenty-four-year veteran of Pennsylvania politics gave the coalition an insider perspective on the levers of power in Harrisburg.

In addition to Cowell's state legislative experience, Donna Cooper, the founding director of Good Schools PA (2000–2003), went on to become Governor Rendell's secretary of policy (2003–2011), giving the campaign an important ally in Harrisburg. Cooper, who is white, is viewed by many in the Philadelphia education community with a mix of awe and apprehension because of her political aptitude and unfiltered speech. She was a key player in pushing Rendell's education agenda forward. As founding director of Good Schools, many of PSFC's school funding goals were aligned with the Rendell administration's goals. According to Michael Churchill, a white attorney with the Public Interest Law Center who is regarded as an elder statesman of school funding, Cooper "carried over her interest in schools and really pushed them hard." By 2007, PSFC had broadened to include almost thirty organizations in its steering committee, and nearly eighty "endorsing organizations"—that is, organizations that provided support but were not responsible for providing direction to the campaign.

Close observers of Pennsylvania politics and education often talk about the years between 2008 and 2011 as the golden years of school funding, however short-lived they were. With Cooper's commitment to school funding, the issue finally became a legislative priority in the governor's office. PSFC, with leadership from ELC, successfully pushed for a costing-out study to determine how much money was needed to have all Pennsylvania students make adequate yearly progress. The vote for the costing-out study was almost unanimously passed by the state legislature. With the introduction of state standards in the 1990s and an accompanying accountability system, the metrics for determining how much it would cost to deliver a "thorough and efficient education" were finally available.

The 2007 study, conducted by an independent company out of Denver, concluded that Pennsylvania needed to increase spending by 25 percent, or the equivalent of $4.38 billion, in order for all students to reach proficiency in the state's learning standards (Augenblick, Palaich and Associates, Inc. 2007). The costing-out study was an opening gambit that then allowed Rendell to argue for a funding target. In addition, Rendell proposed a funding formula that would take the guesswork and politics out of distributing state aid to districts. Though Rendell's formula differed from what was proposed by PSFC, it achieved the same goal: funding that was distributed progressively, with more money going to districts with greater need. Churchill, who was part of those discussions, said the campaign decided that if Rendell's proposal had "the same objective, hell with the details, we'll get behind this."

With a steel-trap memory for details, Churchill recalled that PSFC spent an intense half year, from January 2008 to July 2008, lobbying for Rendell's proposal. In the end, the funding target fell far short of the study's $4.38 billion recommended increase, but the $291 million increase in the state's basic education funding was nevertheless a historic increase. This three-year period would turn out to be a golden era of school funding not only because there was a funding target that provided a historic increase in the state education budget, but also because it was the first time that the state implemented a funding formula since freezing the Equalized Subsidy for Basic Education (ESBE) in 1992. Philadelphia and other majority-minority districts benefited from Rendell's school funding policies. However, because race was hardly ever mentioned, if at all, the strategies used to achieve this historic "win" paved the way for future colorblind tactics.

This golden era came with compromises. According to Rendell's school funding deal, the first year (2008–2009) was funded through state dollars, while the last two years (2009–2011) were funded through the Great Recession's federal stimulus dollars. During the latter two years, federal dollars supplanted state money. When federal money ran out at the end of the 2010–2011 budget year and the new Republican governor, Tom Corbett, refused to restore the loss of funding through state aid, Pennsylvania had a gaping hole in its education budget. Districts across Pennsylvania, but especially places like Philadelphia, suffered tremendously. People in Harrisburg have speculated that supplanting state aid with federal aid was the price that Rendell had to pay to get his funding formula and historic increases to the education budget passed. Though some blame can be assigned to Rendell for making an unsustainable deal, Corbett was no friend of public education. In addition to his refusal to restore the hole in the education budget, he actively promoted vouchers (Worden 2011), which uses taxpayer dollars to pay for private school tuition, and zeroed out the charter school reimbursement line item, effectively forcing school districts to absorb the added costs of charter schools. The narrative—that Corbett cut the state education budget by $1 billion—took hold.

By 2013, PSFC successfully harnessed increased public support for school funding, while Corbett ignored this shift at his own peril. Corbett entered the governorship in 2011, when the Tea Party movement catalyzed western Pennsylvania and members of the state's Republican caucus took the Norquist pledge to not raise taxes. Rendell said Corbett "should have his head examined" (Venkataramanan 2010) for also vowing not to raise taxes, since this meant that there was no new state revenue to plug the hole. Rendell also didn't spare any criticism of state legislators, calling them "scared little rabbits" (Venkataramanan 2010) for their unwillingness to raise taxes. Churchill remembered that "leaders weren't paying any attention to [education]. And they only said, 'Well, everybody's for good schools until they have to pay for it.'" The Republican leadership was still operating under the mistaken belief that Pennsylvanians would oppose new taxes, even at the expense of their schools. That political calculus turned out to be brutally wrong.

When Pennsylvanians were subjected to draconian cuts after Corbett came into office, their priorities had changed. According to a Franklin and Marshall poll, "only four percent of Pennsylvanians considered education the state's most pressing problem [in 2010]" (Kerkstra 2013). But three years later, by September 2013, "education was the top priority in the survey" (Kerkstra 2013). Though the campaign was less active in the immediate years after 2011 due to a gap in grant funding, the infrastructure for organizing against Corbett's cuts already existed. Churchill remarked that PSFC was successful in "convincing the body public that [education] was important because there had been polling for years that said this was important." Moreover, the campaign was able to build on the narrative that Corbett was solely responsible for cutting public education funding by $1 billion. He became the target for the public's discontent about the cuts to education. In 2014, Corbett was voted out of office and became the first Pennsylvania governor in forty years to lose a reelection. This was widely seen as a decisive rebuke of Corbett's cuts to public education.

The Pennsylvania School Funding Campaign boasted several successes during the Rendell golden years (2008–2011), most notably the implementation of a progressive school funding formula, a funding target, and increases to the state education budget. As well, the campaign successfully mobilized people disgruntled over school funding cuts, leading to the ousting of Corbett as a one-term governor. In contrast to Superintendent Hornbeck's approach, which made racial equity a focal point in advocating for school funding, PSFC rarely invoked this, not because its members were blind to racial disparities (after all, Hornbeck was one of the founders of Good Schools PA), but more likely because Hornbeck's race-conscious approach had led to significant setbacks, including the state takeover of Philly schools. Instead, the campaign's strategically colorblind approach yielded some of the most substantial wins, ushering in a brief but golden era of school funding in Pennsylvania. This was not lost on school funding advocates who inherited the mantle years later.

The following chapter focuses on the Campaign for Fair Education Funding (CFEF)—the next iteration of Pennsylvania's school funding campaign. CFEF's decision to take a colorblind advocacy approach was influenced by the lessons learned from the Hornbeck and Rendell eras, and it was swayed by membership-driven organizations (i.e., the ed associations or unions) that were intent on not ruffling the feathers of its members—many of whom were benefiting from hold harmful. Chapter 5 examines the coalitional dynamics in CFEF, with attention to how issues of race get sidelined in the name of speaking in one voice.

### CHAPTER FIVE

# "Speaking with One [Colormute] Voice"

The organizational diversity of the Campaign for Fair Education Funding (CFEF) was a double-edged sword. Bringing together so many groups with a wide range of skills broadened the coalition's message and impact. Ron Cowell, the founder of EPLC and retired Pennsylvania House representative of twenty-four years, captured this idea when he said:

> I think one of the greatest benefits was illustrated by something that I used to frequently identify as a comment from some legislative friends, and they said almost tongue in cheek but practically speaking, "We're not happy with this coalition because you're making it tougher for us. You're all speaking with one voice."

Having so many organizations "speaking with one voice" on issues of school funding was compelling because it "made it tougher for [state legislators]" to ignore such a unified message. But this diversity also pulled the coalition in different directions.

When I asked Cowell about what challenges coalitions face, he demurred to speak critically about the campaign. His measured approach was notable in that at one point in the interview he said: "I've given you a little bit more opinion than I normally would about some of the dynamics." Nevertheless, he offered: "When you ask organizations to work together, typically organizations give up something. You know, it may be time, it may be resources, it may even be some items on their agenda. So that's always a challenge—for organizations to give up something."

Compromise was a necessary and expected part of coalition-building. But from the perspective of race-centered organizations, the campaign's push to speak in "one voice" compromised its ability to talk about *racial* inequities in school funding. These organizations felt like they had to "give up" their race-explicit messaging and conform to being colormute. *Colormuteness* is described as the practice of suppressing race talk in ways that reproduce racial inequities (Pollock 2004) and obscure the *racial* school funding gap. Speaking in one colormute voice can be deeply problematic. It misrepresents the problem to the public and wastes coalitional time and energy on policy solutions that don't address racial inequity in school funding. On a collaborative level, it set the stage for undermining trust among coalitional members, especially between white people and people of color.

Chapter 5 focuses on how colormuteness, and its conceptual relative, colorblindness, enabled white-district domination. State legislators and leaders from the ed associations adamantly protected hold harmful, based on a belief that it is the *natural order of things* for white districts to have more than majority-minority school districts. Though this was never stated explicitly, the mere notion that redistributing state funding in a more equitable way that would benefit Black and Brown districts was anathema to state legislators, especially Republicans. Even their use of the term *hold harmless* reveals how the material well-being of white rural districts is privileged within policymaking considerations. The policy can only be considered "harmless" when viewed from the perspectives of white rural districts. These racial biases were not manifested in the form of racial animus. Rather they were manifested through colorblind policies like hold harmful and the colorblind justification that districts with a net loss of students needed to be protected because of "fixed costs," a "limited tax base," and the need for a "stable level of funding." In emphasizing the benefit of hold harmful to white rural districts, while willfully ignoring its consequences to majority-minority districts, these state legislators and leaders of ed associations practiced a racial double standard, revealing how white-district domination is a settled expectation and the neutral baseline in matters of school funding. Given these individuals' positions of power, the decisions they made upheld Pennsylvania's racist school-funding structure.

## THE CAMPAIGN FOR FAIR EDUCATION
## FUNDING'S "ONE VOICE"

In 2014, the Campaign for Fair Education Funding (CFEF) was launched and included a diverse constituency of "50 business, civic, education, faith-based and nonprofit organizations across the state" (Public Interest Law Center n.d.b). As in previous coalitions, strategic thought was put into inviting organizations to participate. The coalition included organizations that could fortify support and apply pressure in different ways. *Child advocacy organizations,* like the Education Law Center-PA (ELC), the Public Interest Law Center (PILC), and Public Citizens for Children and Youth (PCCY) held webinars, wrote policy reports, and published op-eds to educate the public about the issue of school funding. *Membership-driven education associations* (e.g., Pennsylvania State Education Association (PSEA), Pennsylvania Association of School Business Officials (PASBO), Pennsylvania Association of School Administrators (PASA), and the Pennsylvania School Boards Association (PSBA)) had experience lobbying state legislators and knew the inner workings of Harrisburg. *Community organizing groups* like POWER and the Pennsylvania Immigration and Citizenship Coalition (PICC) mobilized grassroots support, especially within communities of color. Most of the organizations fell into one of these categories, and together, the coalition had data-based expert knowledge on school funding issues, the relationships needed to grease the wheels of change, and grassroots organizing that mobilized public support (see appendix B for a chart on the major players in CFEF and their positions on school funding).

When CFEF convened in 2014, it had a clear and discrete goal that all members signed up for: to press the legislature to pass a school funding formula. Up until that point, Pennsylvania was one of only three states in the country that did not have a formula for distributing state education aid (Education Law Center 2013b). This was embarrassing enough for the state to convene the Basic Education Funding (BEF) Commission in 2014. This bipartisan, bicameral group of fifteen state legislators were appointed to the commission to rectify the state's lack of a funding formula. Eight members of CFEF testified before the commission and presented a united front on a number of issues. Nearly every CFEF member argued three points about a school funding formula: (1) it provided predictability and financial stability to school districts; (2) it should accurately count students; and (3) it should take need into account.

First, campaign members contended that a formula would take the politics out of school funding and provide greater financial stability to school districts. While hold harmful guaranteed a minimum baseline amount, it was widely understood that for many districts, especially those with rising populations since 1991, this minimum was woefully inadequate because of the increased costs of educating more students. The wheeling and dealing to secure earmarked funding for districts was proof of inadequate funding. CFEF called on lawmakers to obviate the need for earmarked funding by making the allocation of state aid less political, and more predictable and transparent for districts through the development of a funding formula.

This is what Joan Benso of Pennsylvania Partnerships for Children (PPC) had in mind when she testified before the commission that school districts needed a "permanent, predictable, financed school funding formula—not one we rejigger every single year when we pass the school code." Earmarked funding often came as a surprise to even superintendents. Though the additional funds were of course welcome, it created budgetary uncertainties from year to year, with superintendents not knowing how much state funding their districts would be allocated in any given year. CFEF fought for school districts to have greater control over their budgets by passing a funding formula that would allow superintendents to know what to expect.

Second, CFEF members all agreed that a funding formula should include accurate and up-to-date information on student populations. Before the adoption of the fair funding formula, the state's school funding structure was based on outdated student population data from 1991. State aid did not recognize changing student enrollment and the increased costs associated with educating more students. The campaign rallied for a basic requirement in the funding formula: count students accurately.

Third, campaign members also felt that a good school funding formula should account for the different needs of districts and students. These additional needs took the form of added "weights" in the formula, and the added weights translated to additional funding.[1] CFEF successfully argued for an English learner weight that took into account the cost of providing a quality education to English learners. Also, the BEF Commission unanimously acted on the campaign's recommendation to institute different weights for poverty. The poverty weights were nuanced and accounted for three levels of poverty: students living in poverty; students living in acute poverty; and students living in a community of concentrated poverty.

Deborah Gordon Klehr, the executive director of the Education Law Center-PA (ELC), recalled this victory as we spoke in her corner office in downtown Philadelphia. She is part of the largest demographic group in the coalition—one that is mostly composed of white women who lead the many nonprofit organizations in the campaign.[2] Klehr is disarmingly friendly with a megawatt smile. Like the well-trained lawyer she is, she often anticipated a counterargument to her own argument. Despite her clear-eyed assessment of the work that remained, the inclusion of the English learner and poverty weights was a definitive "win" for her:

> Those of us who are very involved in the creation of the funding formula initially, and able to get the poverty weights that we were able to get, and the English learner weight, [it] was a huge success— the unanimous support for that in the Commission and the near unanimous support for that in the passage of the [Act].

These weights meant that state aid that went through the formula would be distributed progressively. Almost everyone involved in the creation of the fair funding formula agreed that it was a racially and economically equitable method. In addition to these weights, there was also consideration given to districts with low taxing capacity; districts that had to bear the financial burden of charter schools; and districts with population sparsity (e.g., rural districts that had to pay for fixed costs despite having fewer students and lower tax capacities).

As Ron Cowell said, "speaking with one voice" about an issue "made it tougher for [state legislators]" to deny the issue. In this case, widespread agreement from members of the campaign about the *elements* that should go into a fair funding formula made their message impossible to ignore. The development of a truly fair funding formula—that is, one that did not privilege whiter school districts over majority-minority school districts in the distribution of state aid—was a considerable "win" for CFEF. But the *application* of the fair funding formula, specifically, how much of the education budget to put through the formula and the racial implications of this, would later be a point of contention within the campaign, creating riffs among members.

## PROTECTING WHITE-DISTRICT DOMINATION

By the time I interviewed business casual Dan, the Democratic staffer introduced in an earlier chapter, I had become familiar with the spartan aesthetic of district offices. Unlike the state capitol building in Harrisburg, with its soaring rotunda and gilded ornaments, district offices were homely and, by their sheer appearance, seemed to ward off any accusation of fiscal impropriety. In trying to understand how policies protect white-district domination, it is useful to analyze the discursive moves that state legislators articulate in supporting certain policy proposals over others. In recounting the first Basic Education Funding (BEF) hearing, Dan said that the opening remarks by Republican Representative Donna Oberlander sealed the fate of school funding in Pennsylvania, making both the preservation of hold harmful and the lack of a funding target foregone conclusions.

> The very first statement when the commission gathered was, "We are not going to touch hold harmless." That was established very early, that was the first thing that was said. So the idea that we were going to drive all the money through the formula, the House Republicans swatted that away in the very first statement when the commission met. And so while it was discussed throughout the whole process—"We should do it through the whole thing"—you know, it was never, it was never going to happen. You were never gonna get the votes. Anyone who is participating in the commission knew that that was the case.

While the commission agreed on the necessity of developing a formula for distributing state money, they did not agree on how much funding to put through the formula. To get the formula passed—that is, to get

Republicans to vote "yes"—the bipartisan commission decided to table any serious discussion of getting rid of hold harmful and identifying funding targets. This decision further entrenched existing racial biases in school funding.

The BEF Commission's first hearing occurred in late summer 2014 and had about fifty or so people gathered in one of the senate rooms in Harrisburg. The surroundings resembled a courtroom, formal and restrained. Dark wood paneling covered the walls and rows of wood-trimmed chairs filled the space. It was a room that conveyed order. The cochair of the commission, Senator Pat Browne, a Republican representing Allentown and other parts of the Lehigh Valley, was unavailable that day and had deputized Representative Donna Oberlander to open the proceedings.

A profile of Rep. Oberlander's districts shed light on why she was chosen to stand in for Senator Browne. In 2019–2020, eight out of her ten school districts were "winners," with per-student district windfalls ranging from $2,000 to $5,700; only two of her districts were short-changed ($1,300 and $4,500 per student, respectively). When calculating the wins and losses across all ten school districts, they had a cumulative school funding windfall of $33.6 million. The average poverty rate across ten districts was 22 percent compared to the Philadelphia school district's poverty rate of 35 percent; two of her districts had poverty rates comparable to Philadelphia's at 34 percent and 37 percent. Finally, on average, 96 percent of the students across her districts are white. More to the point, Rep. Oberlander represented districts that were benefiting from hold harmful, and selecting her to open the proceeding, to give her perspective, foreclosed any possibility of abolishing hold harmful.

Lest any unspoken expectations went unheeded, Representative Oberlander's opening remarks included a statement of her goals and her expressed commitment to "guard against a new formula that hurts districts that have justifiably relied on the hold harmless provision." Presiding over the hearing like a judge, she was steady, resolute, and dispassionate. She lifted her eyes every now and then as she read from her prepared statement:

We all know, we live in a diverse commonwealth and our citizens' interests are different depending on if we live in a rural, suburban, or urban area, and whether school districts are growing or losing students, or whether our school districts have strong tax bases or shrinking tax bases. Above all, however, the goal of the House Republican Caucus is fairness for school districts and taxpayers of the commonwealth. This commission's charge is not to study [the] so-called adequate level of basic education funding. The responsibility of determining a funding level belongs to the General Assembly and is based each year on overall state revenues. This commission cannot tie the General Assembly to funding targets. Rather this commission's charge is to determine a formula for distributing basic education funding in a fair and equitable manner. And we all know, our basic education funding formulas have, for many years, included what is known as a hold harmless to ensure no district receives revenues less than the previous years. The hold harmless is important to many school districts, including my own. Rural school districts, like other school districts, serve as community centers. This function is important, but the basic costs of keeping the building open and keeping the lights on are fixed. School districts depend on a stable level of funding to help pay these fixed costs. In a rural district with a limited tax base, state support is needed to help school districts fulfill this vital function for their communities. While the commission will be examining the hold harmless, I will guard against a new formula that hurts districts that have justifiably relied on the hold harmless provision. I look forward to taking part in this commission's work as it unfolds over the next several months.

Representative Oberlander began her statement by mentioning how "diverse [our] commonwealth and our citizens' interests are." The kind of diversity she wished to highlight though was not racial, ethnic, or linguistic diversity, but rather, geographic (i.e., "rural, suburban, or urban") and economic (i.e., "strong tax bases or shrinking tax bases") diversity. Interestingly, she also treated districts with declining student populations as a form of diversity, mentioning that some school districts were "growing" while others were "losing students." Here, she sidestepped any mention of race, but appropriated the language of diversity to advocate for the needs of districts like her own—rural, predominantly white districts with a shrinking tax base, and a declining student population.

The language of "diversity," entrenched in institutional discourse since the 1990s, is often mobilized to call for greater inclusion of groups that have suffered societal marginalization. Diversity claims are one way of rectifying historical wrongs, though it has also been a way of managing dissent (Ahmed 2012). One aspect of Representative Oberlander's usage of diversity is aligned with this broader understanding of righting wrongs, as she immediately follows up the appeal to diversity with an appeal to "fairness," which is "above all . . . the goal of the House Republican Caucus." While geographic (e.g., rural) and economic (e.g., taxable wealth) marginalization is consistent with the purposes of diversity discourses, declining student population is inconsistent with what we usually consider to be a diversity issue.

By commingling declining student population with geographic and economic marginalization, Representative Oberlander attempted to legitimize the issue of declining student numbers as a diversity issue and to confer to those school districts the material resources that often accompany diversity claims. Her diversity claim was intended to help her school districts maintain their share of state aid. To her, defending the right of her school districts to keep their share of school funding, despite having fewer students to educate, was an issue of "fairness." But the kind of "fairness" she advocates is one that comes at the expense of other school districts with increasing student populations, like those serving majority-poor students of color. There is a deep irony that should be noted here: she co-opted the language of diversity, most notably used by people of color and other marginalized groups to make claims to institutional resources they have been systematically excluded from, in order to claim financial resources for her own districts that have benefited from Pennsylvania's outdated school funding scheme for decades—all in the name of "fairness."

By noting that the "commission's charge is not to study [the] so-called adequate level of basic education," Representative Oberlander made the issue of school funding a zero-sum game that pitted rural white districts against majority-minority urban districts—one in which most of her school districts came out as winners. The injunction—"this commission cannot tie the General Assembly to funding targets"—created an untenable situation for school districts with increasing student populations by foreclosing any chance of increasing school funding to adequate levels. Representative Oberlander continued her remarks by reinforcing the policy of hold harmful. She noted that "hold harmless is important to many school districts including my own" and then issued a second injunction, promising to "guard against a new formula that hurts districts that have justifiably relied on the hold harmless provision." By preserving hold harmful, her school districts stood to keep their $33.6 million windfall. This ever-active stasis protected the school funding status quo and maintained white-district domination.

The double injunction issued by Rep. Oberlander—to preserve hold harmful and to not tie the General Assembly to funding targets—meant that the BEF Commission, from its inception, consigned school districts like Philadelphia, Reading, Allentown, and Lancaster—districts that educate significant numbers of poor and nonwhite students—to an inequitable portion of existing funds and to funding levels that were not adequate to meeting the state's own learning standards. To her, majority-white districts maintaining their $33.6 million windfall was "fair." Representative Rabb, the Philly-based state lawmaker whose House Bill 961 proposed to put 100 percent of the money through the fair funding formula, said: "If you haven't been operating fairly for generations . . . what is normal is actually unfair to you." David Mosenkis from POWER conveyed a similar sentiment when he recited this quote: "When you're accustomed to privilege, equality feels like oppression."[3]

Laws, funding formulas, and the notion of "fair" were subjective and biased, and as one state legislator admitted, they could be "tweak[ed]" to benefit some districts over others. As someone involved in the 2016 decisions, he had this to say about funding formulas:

> It depends on my perspective as to what I think is important, and who I think I'm representing, and why I should care about anyone else, and you know . . . as a legislator, I can tweak them in my mind to anything I want them to be. I think the research would show differently, but in this day and age, when facts and science and you know, statistical research and things, are like, "Who cares? It's what I think that matters," it's a sort of scary prospect to think how you could basically flip one of these fair funding formulas to the point where it wasn't fair, and you could claim that you were being fair about it.

Based on his experiences, this state legislator saw how a politician's "perspective" on funding was shaped by who they were "representing." It is noteworthy that he talked about the role of a legislator in competitive terms: "who I think I'm representing" makes a legislator question "why [I should] care about anyone else." He saw how a politician's "perspective" could allow them to "flip one of these fair funding formulas" in a way that went against "research," "facts and science," but still be able to "claim that you were being fair about it."

Similarly, a Democratic Ohio representative used the term *fudged the formula* to refer to the power state legislators have in driving money out to districts they have a vested interest in protecting. He talked about a community that lost two power plants and his dedication to protecting local taxpayers from having to make up the lost revenue from the plant closures, and the Faustian bargains he had to make in the process. He succinctly stated: "We fudged the formula to drive more money to those districts that were losing power plants. But what that meant . . . is that we took away from other districts [that] really could have used it."

In the marketplace of ideas, not all perspectives hold equal footing when it comes to translating those perspectives into law and policy. The perspectives of Republican BEF Commission members held the most sway because, as business casual Dan explained, "the Republicans control both chambers and really don't necessarily have to involve Democrats to get votes to pass something." As a law, hold harmful, which was protected by Republican BEF Commission members and Republican leadership, "recognized and protected expectations grounded in white privilege" (Harris 1993:1731). Rep. Oberlander's defense of hold harmful is indexical of how white-district domination "became tantamount to property that could not permissibly be intruded upon without consent" (Harris 1993:1731).

If we think of whiteness-as-property as the settled expectation of keeping $33.6 million more than your fair share, because it is protected by law, and because majority-white legislators create the laws, then defendants of hold harmful simply see themselves protecting their property and what they are legally entitled to. Privilege allows one to only consider "who I think I'm representing"; to question "why [I should] care about anyone else"; and to neglect the effects of policies on others. Oberlander did not mention the effects of hold harmful on districts that have suffered because of this law. Representative democracy gives her an easy out: after all, she was elected to protect the interests of her own (majority-white) constituents who would lose out if the school funding structure changed. Cheryl Harris (1993:1731) argues that "when the law recognizes . . . the settled expectations of whites . . . it acknowledges and reinforces a property interest in whiteness that reproduces Black subordination." Hold harmful reinforced the property rights of white students while subordinating the interests of Black and Brown students.

## WHEN COLORBLINDNESS DOMINATES THE AGENDA

The fissures between coalition members within CFEF started to become evident during the BEF Commission hearings in 2014 and mainly centered on the issue of race. The ed associations that had closer relationships to state legislators and were resistant to talking about race were invited to speak at length to the commission. Community organizers from POWER, who wanted to draw attention to racial inequities, were shut out of the process and had to fight for an opportunity to testify.

With skillful storytelling ability, Bishop Dwayne Royster recounted POWER's fight for a timeslot during the BEF Commission hearing to a group of POWER's volunteer organizers who listened with rapt attention. Bishop Royster, who is Black, is the executive director of POWER. He set up the story beginning with the antagonists: "Pat Browne and Mike Vereb," he said, "both conservatives," were members of the BEF Commission. They had hearings throughout the commonwealth, but testifying was by invitation only. David Mosenkis, who is Jewish and whose synagogue is part of POWER, was set up as one of the protagonists. David, a professional data scientist who later became the leader of POWER's statewide education team, had recently published his 2014 findings that revealed a clear racial bias in the way state education funding was distributed. POWER leaders were keen to share these findings with the commission, and in keeping with their mantra, they wanted parents and community members who were "closest to the pain" to testify. As Bishop Royster said, "We had things we wanted to share, but [Senator Browne] said 'No,' and wouldn't allow us to testify during the hearing."

Bishop Royster told this next part of the story to underscore a principle of organizing work: "We don't win if we don't increase tension." POWER's education team turned up the heat by issuing a press release with the following demand: if David Mosenkis doesn't testify, we're shutting down the hearing. The news media called Senator Browne's office to get a comment, and shortly after, Browne relented. With the senator's tail between his legs, someone from his office called POWER. Bishop Royster reenacted the person on the other end of the line, capturing the staffer's forced dignity: "We understand that you're going to testify." Royster's comical delivery was met with raucous laughter. In the end, David spoke to the commission for fifteen minutes and raised the issue of racial inequity in school funding. Philadelphia parents and community members took about forty minutes to share about their experiences of underfunding, and the commission promised to allocate spots to parents and community members for future hearings across the state. This story was retold by Bishop Royster along with a quote by Frederick Douglass, "Power concedes nothing without a demand," as a reminder that conflict and tension can be productive.

But the story also underscores which organizations in CFEF had the ear of the BEF Commission, how CFEF chose to use their political capital, and the colorblind tactics they used to defend the interests of white rural districts. POWER fought tooth and nail for David to speak for fifteen minutes, while representatives of member-driven education associations in CFEF, all of whom are white men, were invited to testify and allotted considerably more time to speak to the commission. Michael Crossey (former president) and Eric Elliott (director of research), representing the Pennsylvania State Education Association (PSEA)— the state's teachers' union—talked for twenty-two minutes. Jay Himes, the executive director of the Pennsylvania Association of School Business Officials (PASBO), spoke at not one, but *two* hearings. In one of those hearings, Himes and Jim Buckheit, the executive director of the Pennsylvania Association of School Administrators (PASA), spoke for nearly two hours. Joan Benso, of Pennsylvania Partnerships for Children (PPC), which is not a union but has close ties to state legislators, spoke for thirty-four minutes. The second-longest time (nearly one hour) was allotted to Ron Cowell, perhaps not only because of his deep knowledge of issues of school funding, but also because he was considered one of their own as a former representative in the Pennsylvania House. The allotted times reflected which organizations and people were valued by the BEF Commission in making decisions about school funding, and how their perspectives dominated the agenda. Notably, the people who directly bear the impact of Pennsylvania's school funding system did not occupy a privileged place before the commission.

The testimonies given by the ed associations reflected their desire to protect white rural districts. In the nearly two-hour testimony given by Jim Buckheit (PASA) and Jay Himes (PASBO), they spent considerable time explaining "Basic Education Funding 101," including providing descriptive statistics of districts and student populations. Buckheit informed the commission that there are 253 rural districts. These rural districts make up 47 percent of districts in Pennsylvania even though they only educate 26 percent of Pennsylvania's students. What Buckheit left out were the racial demographics of these small rural districts: 96 percent of its students are white. To disarm dissent, Buckheit rhetorically asked why so many resources were spent on so few students:

> Why would you operate a building that small? Well, the reasoning comes down to, you can't have a six-year-old student sitting in a bus for an hour and half going to and from school each day. It's just not the right thing to do. So you have to operate schools that are less than cost-efficient.

Buckheit reasoned that there were extenuating circumstances that justified a "less than cost-efficient" approach to funding schools. Moreover, by telling the story of a six-year-old enduring a one-and-a-half-hour bus ride, Buckheit humanizes the problem of taking money away from white rural districts.

He was essentially arguing that some circumstances should override economies of scale considerations; the *moral* economy of educating students should also be considered—"you can't have a six-year-old student sitting in a bus for an hour and half going to and from school each day. *It's just not the right thing to do*" (emphasis added). Agreed. And yet it should be noted that no such nuanced considerations are made for majority-Black-and-Brown urban school districts that are regularly attacked for their so-called inefficient spending. Recall the comment made by Governor Ridge's spokesperson to Superintendent Hornbeck when he asked for more money for Philadelphia: "Hornbeck has not successfully focused on the first step of this equation, which is how Philadelphia's schools are spending the money they have now" (Tabor 1996). More "efficient" spending would not resolve a problem that begins with the state shortchanging Philadelphia out of $400 million each year. Policymakers in Harrisburg imposed a racial double standard: for white rural school districts, special consideration of their circumstances should be made, but majority-minority urban school districts should be more "efficient" with their spending.

Displaying a similar impulse to protect funding to white rural districts, Jay Himes spoke about the "aid ratios"—an index that calculates the proportion of state aid a school district should receive based on local wealth factors (e.g., income, market value of taxable property). He presented a list that showed how some school districts (i.e., white rural ones) were trending toward a lower aid ratio, which might seem to suggest they were getting wealthier and in less need of state education aid. Lest the untrained eye come to any specious conclusions, Himes editorialized about this:

> Now I would sort of defy you to be able to explain on this list how any of these districts is really getting wealthier. I would suspect they're not getting wealthier at all. I would suspect they're losing student population. So if you went back to that calculation I showed you previously, I believe it's all in the math. It's not in the district, it's not in the kids, it's not in their finances, it's all in the math. Because you take less students, you spread out the same wealth, in terms of either income or market value, I believe, "Voila," you create a 'richer' looking district even though none of those financial factors in that district would lead you to believe they're getting richer. These are mostly small, very rural, except for the last one, districts that would be trending from higher to lower aid ratios.

Himes explained the lower aid ratio of white rural districts to defend them. He defied anyone to show how "any of these districts is really getting wealthier." His argument was basically: if the dividend (i.e., wealth) remains the same, but the divisor (i.e., student population) decreases, then "'Voila,' you create a 'richer' looking district." According to Himes, the "calculation" and "math" distort the financial reality of white rural districts, much like fun house mirrors distort one's reflection. He explained this to provide a fuller context of the situation so the BEF Commission could see that these districts were not getting "richer" and to convince them not to reduce aid. Like Buckheit, Himes went to great lengths to contextualize the predicament of white rural districts, but no such contextualization is afforded to students in majority-minority school districts.

Like Rep. Oberlander in the opening remarks, Buckheit and Himes took a colorblind approach that avoided any mention of race. Himes specifically mentioned that these were "mostly small" and "very rural" districts to signify their low economic status, but he neglected to mention that 96 percent of the students who benefit from his defense of them are white. If the unmarked category—that is, what is so taken for granted that it needs no mention—is often aligned with the attributes of the speaker, then the elision of these districts' whiteness serves as an unmarked category that is aligned with Himes's own whiteness. Just because race is not explicitly stated, doesn't mean race is irrelevant. In fact, quite the opposite. Just as the term *welfare mom* makes no mention of race (or age), yet people in the United States understand this to be "code for African American inner-city teenage mother" (Kingfisher 2007:95), so white districts served as the unmarked category in policy discussions that sought to protect hold harmful. The erasure of race in matters of school funding demonstrates how naturalized white-district domination is—it needs no explicit mention, and it is reflexively defended by state legislators and school funding advocates alike.

## HOW POLITICAL CAPITAL IS USED TO REINFORCE WHITE-DISTRICT DOMINATION

The fact that leaders of the ed associations in CFEF were willfully colorblind was problematic, to say the least. But what made it dangerous was that they had the most political clout in the coalition and used that power to shape the campaign's agenda to protect white-district domination. Although the unions were brought into the coalition to leverage their preexisting relationships with state legislators, they were calculative about how they used their political capital and careful to not be too "rash."

John Callahan, the white chief advocacy officer for PSBA, explained some of the challenges of being part of the coalition. "So, I always say, you know, my only job is that I have to negotiate on the hill, and sometimes advocacy organizations don't have to do that." Callahan contrasted "elected members [who] go into office and have a discussion about issues" with other groups that "go up to the capitol and kind of bang drums and protest in front of offices." The organizing groups, he said, "can be a little more rash than an association could be." He added: "I have to continue to have relationships with people that are long-lasting, and then when you're looking at it, you know, today you might not get a vote, but tomorrow you may get a vote, so those relationships are very important in order to keep and get things done." While these "long-lasting" relationships created inroads for the ed associations, it also barred them from advocating for issues that would upset the relational status quo with state politicians. They didn't want to jeopardize votes down the road (e.g., pension, teacher evaluations) for issues that many of their members didn't consider to be as important (e.g., racially equitable school funding).

Keeping all five hundred school districts happy and engaged was critical to the financial health of the ed associations since membership dues were a primary source of revenue. Because of this, the interests of their (predominantly white) members superseded the interest of advocating for equitable school funding. According to a former CFEF participant, the unions were "more easily distracted than others." That was why the William Penn Foundation, which funded the work of these campaigns, tended to select non-member-based organizations to lead these coalitions. While Pennsylvania Partnerships for Children (PPC) is not a union, it held a similar perspective as the unions—it didn't want to spend its political currency on transforming the school funding system. Their advocacy issues included early learning, child welfare, health care, home visitations, and K–12 education.[4] PPC's broad agenda included but was certainly not limited to K–12 funding.

Since racial inequity in school funding was seen as a fringe or nonissue by union members, it wasn't a priority for the ed associations.

Characterizing the position of the unions and PPC, the former CFEF participant explained, they don't want to be "so aggressive that [they] burn bridges or somehow diminish relationships [with state legislators] because today you may be asking for support for K–12 funding but tomorrow you may have any number of other items on your agenda." Advocating for racial equity in school funding meant supporting a plan to redistribute funding—a position that the unions felt pitted members against each other and would have made for disgruntled dues-paying members. Representative Oberlander maintained white-district domination when she prioritized her majority-white constituents by promising to "guard against a new formula that hurts districts that have justifiably relied on the hold harmless provision." For their part, the unions reinforced the racial school funding status quo when they prioritized the happy engagement of their predominantly white members, who make up the majority of their membership, over their few Black and Latine school district members.

## AN EMPTY PROMISE TO FIX RACIAL INEQUITY IN SCHOOL FUNDING

In contrast to Buckheit and Himes, who represented the ed associations from CFEF, David Mosenkis, representing POWER, spoke explicitly about the racial bias in the state's distribution of education funding during one of the BEF Commission's hearings. This took place a few months after Buckheit's and Himes's testimonies, and only after POWER organizers applied significant pressure on Senator Browne and threatened to shut down the hearing if David and parents weren't allowed to speak. To try to lighten the mood of the otherwise stiff and formal proceedings, Senator Browne lightly joked about the benefit of holding the hearing in southeastern Pennsylvania rather than western New York that got blanketed with seventy-four inches of snow in twenty-four hours. On the day that David came before the BEF Commission to testify, he was flanked by about twenty or so POWER members who sat in the public gallery of one of Philadelphia's City Hall courtrooms. He was one of the last to testify as a late addition to the agenda.

David opened his testimony with a summary of his findings: "My analysis," he said, "reveals a dramatic pattern of racial inequity in the way our state's districts are funded, whereby districts with predominantly white students receive significantly higher basic education funding per student than economically similar districts with more minority students." Then, like the seasoned data scientist he is, David walked the audience through each of his graphs, translating complex information in digestible ways. He talked about one piece of "good news" in Pennsylvania funding: the higher the poverty level, the more basic education funding a district received per student. Shifting to a more ominous tone, he delivered the main thesis of his testimony:

> But a disturbing trend emerges when we color the districts by their racial composition. . . . What's shocking is the racial pattern we see in these graphs. The whiter the district, the further above the line it is. The greater the portion of minority students, the further below the line a district tends to be.

To put these statistics into terms that people would understand, he gave an example: in districts with 50 to 60 percent poverty, whiter districts receive an average of about $6,200 per student compared to $3,600 for less-white districts. These dramatic disparities in funding exist at all poverty levels between whiter and less-white districts. His findings confirmed what Black and Latine families have intuitively known all along: structural racism exists in education funding.

David closed his testimony with careful wording that avoided directly assigning individual blame, while also conveying the urgency of the issue. He said:

> Surely this commission would never design a funding formula with the intention to systematically discriminate against districts based on the race of their students. Probably the same is true of the legislature that approved the current funding levels. Yet in our complex environment, racial discrimination can emerge even without intention. . . . Now that we are aware of it, we cannot afford to let the current systematic racial bias continue for even one more year.

David's speech act can be analyzed in a few ways. On its surface, he was simply communicating his belief that the commission and the legislature "would never design a funding formula with the intention to systematically discriminate against districts based on the race of their students." But as linguists will tell you, there's a difference between what is said, what is meant, and the result of the utterance (Austin 1962).

David's speech act about the commission and the state legislature was more than just a statement of belief. By calling them out, he was also trying to compel them to act, as the last sentence suggests: "Now that we are aware of [the racial discrimination], we cannot afford to let the current systemic racial bias continue even for one more year." While the statement of belief ("Surely this commission would never design . . .") seems to refuse to label state legislators as "racists," the illocutionary force of the speech act is more complex. David was essentially issuing a directive: *You've just been presented with irrefutable evidence that the school funding structure is racially discriminatory. If you don't want to be called a racist after knowing this information, then do something about it.*

Senator Browne understood the underlying meaning of David's closing statement and his immediate response was what one might expect of politicians in public settings: a promise to do better. He said:

> I think you're reinforcing the fact that you don't ever want your formulas, especially those you . . . don't update over time, to have any unintended consequences, because at a minimum it sends the bad public policy message, a bad overall message and there's no reason in regards to what we do in the future that should continue to allow that even to be considered from an unintended consequence. So, that type of information coming forward to us is important so that we, in going forward, not only consider financial implications but the larger implications of what our formulas do. So David, thank you very much for your help.

To absolve himself and others of the racial disparities in school funding that David had just laid bare, Senator Browne talked about the "unintended consequences" of not updating formulas. By mentioning "unintended consequences," he was pleading ignorance to how the state's education funding policy systematically shortchanged majority-minority districts. However, his remark—"So, that type of information coming forward to us is important so that we, in going forward, not only consider financial implications but the larger implications of what our formulas do"—seemed to have the effect that David had hoped for: a commitment to make the school funding system racially equitable. And yet, this not only turned out to be an empty promise, but Senator Browne *knew* that the commission would not rectify the racial bias in school funding even as he sat there and made a pledge to consider "the larger implications of what our formulas do."

By the time David testified in November 2014, the BEF Commission had already held its first hearing months prior in August 2014. During the very first hearing, Senator Browne deputized Rep. Oberlander to deliver opening remarks to make clear the intention of preserving hold harmful. Although the BEF Commission's final report left open the possibility of returning to a debate about hold harmful, the legislature eventually decided to preserve hold harmful *and* to not identify a funding target. The decision to maintain hold harmful would make even the fairest of fair funding formulas functionally ineffective, while the decision to not identify a funding target meant that not only were the slices of pie distributed unfairly, but the pie itself was too small to make any difference. As cochair of the commission, Senator Browne demonstrated willful neglect of racial disparities in state education aid. Even as he expressed concern and a desire to fix the problem of racial bias in Pennsylvania school funding during the November 2014 hearing, he knew that this would be impossible given the commission's commitment to preserving hold harmful and its refusal to identify a funding target expressed during the first hearing in August 2014. When faced with hard evidence of the racial school funding gap, Senator Browne and the rest of the commission exercised choices to preserve Pennsylvania's racist school-funding system.

Shortly after the General Assembly passed Act 35 in 2016, which instituted a new fair funding formula but also preserved hold harmful, the understanding of what this meant for students of color in financially struggling districts came to light. Sherif El-Mekki (2016), a graduate of Philadelphia public schools and principal of Mastery Charter School, wrote:

> Your child's per pupil funding will largely depend on the hue of the students in your district. No surprises there, but when a commission

is created to determine equitable funding, you don't expect them
to equitably distribute only about 6 percent of the pot so brazenly.
I admit, I was naively, albeit, cautiously, optimistic. Shame on me.

When El-Mekki admitted to his naive optimism, he was referring to the
mistaken belief of many that the fair funding formula would be applied
to the entire pot of state education money. Because of the decision to
drive only new money through the formula—an amount that was insufficient to meet the educational needs of students—the BEF Commission's
work did little to change the actual conditions of teaching and learning
in school districts that are the most severely underfunded. The fact that
student funding depended on the "hue of the students in the district"
was "no surprise" to him. It's a tale as old as time, with a predictable
punchline. Upon understanding that not much would change, even after
the adoption of the fair funding formula, El-Mekki disparaged himself
for momentarily believing otherwise. State legislators had found another
way to re-entrench racial hierarchy in school funding. His frustration was
shared by organizers in POWER who dared to hope that things would
be different this time. El-Mekki (2016) continued to say:

> State Republicans are quick to denounce anyone who calls them
> racist, despite the fact that they control the legislature and there
> is a clear pattern of racist distribution of state education funding.
> David Mosenkis (who wrote the POWER report) said, "There are a
> lot of ways that racism manifests itself in our society . . . and a lot of
> them are not because individuals are consciously racist or making
> decisions to consciously underserve or discriminate against people
> of color." But once systemic racism is clearly pointed out and you
> refuse to do anything about it, what are you?

What made David Mosenkis's findings a game-changer was that it denied state legislators the ability to plead ignorance to racial disparities
in school funding. It exposed the agentive structural racism state lawmakers practiced through willful neglect of racial equity. Structural
racism doesn't have magical powers—it is upheld one policy decision at
a time. This pointed question posed by El-Mekki should eat at all state
legislators, the governor, and advocates of school funding who have

helped to maintain a racially stratified system of school funding. "Once systemic racism is clearly pointed out and you refuse to do anything about it, what are you?"

## A STRATEGIC COLORBLIND "WIN"

Despite the limitations of Act 35, CFEF heralded the development of a fair funding formula as a decisive victory for Pennsylvania children. Campaign leaders gathered on the steps of 440 North Broad (the School District of Philadelphia's central office) on a cloudy day in late April 2016 to mark the occasion. The speakers engaged in a delicate two-step that highlighted the groundbreaking work of the coalition in attaining a fair funding formula, while also drawing attention to the work that remained. In celebrating the passage of the fair funding formula, Susan Spicka, executive director of Education Voters PA (considered to be one of the more progressive white-led organizations within the campaign), remarked on how the formula put an end to the practice of earmarked funding: "We are pleased that the era of backroom deals that delivered new school funding to schools with politically powerful members of the legislature has ended." Donna Cooper, of PCCY (formerly Governor Rendell's secretary of policy), stated:

> Our powerful statewide coalition has a demonstrated track record of success, and we agree that we must now get the legislature to fund the formula so that we finally end the curse of a child's zip code determining the public education quality in Pennsylvania. We succeeded once and we will succeed again.

The imperative mood of Cooper's statement—"we must now get the legislature to fund the formula"—referred to the decision to selectively apply the formula to only new money. To better achieve the intended effect of the funding formula—that is, distributing school funding in a more equitable manner—Cooper and others called for significant increases to the education budget so that more money would be driven through the progressive formula. CFEF proposed an increase of $400 million to the state education budget (Public Citizens for Children and Youth 2016).

Among the things that people mentioned about Cooper was her ability to distill complicated information in ways that mattered to people, and her fine-tuned ability to pivot according to her audience, including on matters of race. By mobilizing the zip code trope, her political skills were on full display. Referring to "the curse of a child's zip code" did double-duty for Cooper: (1) to her in-person audience—Philadelphia progressives who cared about matters of race and inequality—it signaled the injustices of racial segregation; (2) to an audience of Harrisburg politicians, who are allergic to talking about race, it was colorblind discourse; it simply referred to geography and economic background.

This strategic colorblind approach was borne out of an astute reading of the political tea leaves. As Rendell's former secretary of policy, Cooper knew that Democrats faced a backlash after Rendell's governorship. Recall business casual Dan's comment: "No one could get anything moved that had the word 'Rendell' attached to it." She understood that the argument of racial inequity in school funding and touting the added weights in the new formula as a great benefit for *Philadelphia* could create a backlash for years to come. This was what Cooper's colleagues meant when they talked about her political acumen. She understood the kind of maneuvering that happened in the state legislature and crafted her message accordingly—a message that could be interpreted in multiple ways, especially in ways that catered to her audience's brand of racial politics. Her speech acts left room for plausible deniability.

Yet as one of her campaign colleagues made clear, Cooper did not always rely on colorblind zip code tropes; she strategically pivoted between "racially explicit" messaging and a "race-neutral strategy."

I think she recognizes the value of having more racially explicit progressive messaging in mobilization work and does that. . . . But in a campaign context, she will never do that. I think probably in the back of her mind, she may be thinking, "Okay, how do I get more money to these districts?" And well, even, like it took me a while to realize this about her, but like because she knows the ed associations' angle and the legislators' angle, she is definitely of the mind that you find the white districts that are going to, that also have some of the same issues or same characteristics, so it's a race-neutral strategy. You do those kinds of things even if the goal has a racial equity aim; you do it in a race-neutral way.

Cooper "recognize[d] the value" of more racially explicit messaging for mobilizing progressives because that kind of messaging was infused with the emotive force of fighting for racial "justice" and "equity." Talking about Black and Brown children had visceral, sensorial, and affective appeal.

Kamari Clarke (2019:47) refers to *affective justice* as "the embodied and regimented assemblages of practices by which people make sense of and project their understandings of justice." These constructions of justice and equity rely on "practices of seeing race (or presuming not to see it) [and] are central to shaping . . . affective landscapes" (Clarke 2019:47). Here, the affective landscape—the terrain in which people have the "capacity to affect and to be affected" (Massumi 1987:xvii)—was comprised of two forms of equity: a multiracial, colorblind notion of equity; and a historically informed, race-conscious understanding of equity. Cooper's distinctiveness was her deft ability to know what the situation called for, to maneuver the affective landscape, and to strategically deploy the right form of equity for the right audience, in the right moment.

As her campaign colleague explained, "In a campaign context, she will never do that" because she knows "the ed associations' angle and the legislators' angle . . . even if the goal has a racial equity aim, you do it in a race-neutral way." This strategic race-neutral approach was indicative of the campaign's modus operandi. Though the more progressive, equity-minded organizations within the coalition would sometimes mention the impact of unequal funding on *students of color*, especially when fundraising, CFEF carefully excluded race-based language from its materials. None of its promotional materials, webpages, newsletter communications reference the *racial* gap in school funding or how *Black* and *Latine* students bore the brunt of state underfunding.

When Cooper proclaimed, "We succeeded once and we will succeed again," she was harkening back to the 2008–2011 golden era of school funding and her accomplishments as Rendell's secretary of policy in establishing the Rendell funding formula and increasing the education budget—accomplishments that were won through colorblind tactics. CFEF's strategy of sidelining race was bolstered by a history that gave school funding advocates their most significant gains during Rendell's golden, but colorblind, era of school funding, and their most significant losses during Hornbeck's race-confrontational period as superintendent.

The campaign's unwillingness to touch the sacred cow of hold harmful, which protects white-district domination, was largely dictated by the ed associations who were the most politically powerful groups within the campaign. While CFEF relied on their political capital to make the campaign viable, the ed associations were not willing to spend that capital on advancing the issue of racial equity in school funding. Instead, they wanted to save it for issues they thought their members cared more about, like pension and teacher evaluation issues. Despite having organizations within CFEF that were politically connected, this did little to change the racial school funding status quo. The stance of the ed associations essentially mirrored Senator Browne's, who preserved hold harmful and refused to identify a funding target at the outset of the BEF Commission's hearings.

*What are the costs associated with taking a colorblind approach?* I asked Cooper's campaign colleague this question. She answered that Cooper's view is that "if the alternative is nothing, which would be the result if you were to do it in a racial explicit way, or something by doing it in a race-neutral way, it's better to do something." In other words, it's better to declare some kind of "win," than no win at all. While the campaign undoubtedly derived strength from "speaking with one [colormute] voice," this process led to an anodyne message, distilled to basic issues that everyone could agree upon like the development of a fair funding formula (not its application) and increasing the state education budget. The campaign's unified message meant that the voices of groups like POWER were muted in the campaign. It also meant that the issue of racial inequity in school funding was made invisible, with CFEF framing the problem as that of inadequate resources and economic inequality. While the development of the fair funding formula was celebrated by all groups as a significant "win," the colorblind framing of the issue was a missed opportunity to build public support to dismantle Pennsylvania's persistent legacy of racism in school funding and to keep state legislators and the governor accountable for their parts in preserving a racially unequal system of school funding.

Leaders of the ed associations not only used their political capital to protect white-district domination, but as chapter 6 demonstrates, they, along with others, also actively silenced dissenting voices within the coalition and actively buried the issue of racial equity. The next chapter provides an intimate look at the breakup of the Campaign for Fair Education Funding, including the ousting of POWER, one of the few Black-led organizations in the coalition. By telling this story, I highlight how a coalition formed out of organizations with not only divergent skill sets but, more importantly, with wildly divergent perspectives on race was designed to fail.

# CHAPTER SIX
# Displacing Racial Equity

"There's definitely been just straight up conflict over that."

Sundrop Carter, the white executive director of the Pennsylvania Immigration and Citizenship Coalition (PICC), told me this with unguarded frankness. "That" referred to the racial justice goals of PICC—an approach that other member organizations in the Campaign for Fair Education Funding (CFEF), especially the ed associations, chafed at. As the interview continued, her self-possessed composure took the stifled formality out of the process, putting my students and I at ease. "PICC as an organization," she said, "we really hold up values of racial justice and inclusivity, and that those most impacted should lead the work."

Similarly, Carter described POWER as an organization that understands "when we are talking about equity, we're talking about [how] there is a history of Black communities being underfunded and segregation still exists in our education system. *Brown v. Board* is not fully realized." As she continued, she fluidly slipped between describing POWER's orientation and the use of an imperative "we," suggesting alignment between the two organizations. "We have to approach that head on and talk about racial inequality when we're talking about fair funding." But the third rail of race was a topic that many members in CFEF wanted to avoid, and it served as a source of conflict.

"So, some of these [ed associations], they just see it as kind of . . ." I paused for Carter to fill in the blank.

"It's like a budget fight," she responded on cue. She pointedly summarized the differences in the following way:

I think there's some people who are like, "We need to talk about education funding as part of the history of racial segregation in this country, and we need to acknowledge that and move forward." And some people are like, "We just need $4 billion. Let's just get that and we'll be fine."

These two framings of the school funding problem—one that focused on *racial inequity* in school funding, the other on getting *more money* into the education budget—characterized two different approaches within CFEF and the priorities of the two different campaigns (i.e., POWER and PA Schools Work) that emerged after CFEF disbanded. While these were not mutually exclusive positions (several organizations including POWER and some of the most progressive groups in PA Schools Work advocated for *both* increases to the state education budget and redistribution), in school funding shorthand, these stances can be typified as a fight for *racial equity* and a fight for *adequacy*.

This chapter is about the "straight up conflict" that ensued between members of CFEF because of their stances on school funding; conflict that culminated in POWER being kicked out. I conduct a postmortem analysis of the campaign's demise to argue that coalitions based on bringing unlikely bedfellows together, particularly those with extremely divergent views on race, is a design flaw that leads to failure on two accounts. First, it failed on ethical grounds by allowing more powerful members of the coalition to drive out an organization because of its commitment to centering race in the campaign. Second, the coalition was just ineffective, stuck in political gridlock over their different stances on school funding or putting forth proposals that did little to address inequity.

Most of the organizations within CFEF and their orientation to school funding can be categorized in one of three ways. The first is what Erica Turner (2020) refers to as the "social justice racial project" that promotes "race consciousness [as] an emancipatory effort to recognize racial differences, racial identity, racial inequality, and racial hierarchy so as to address persistent and deeply entrenched racial inequity" (Turner 2020:24). The work of POWER and PICC fell into this category. POWER's policy position was informed by its goal of abolishing racial bias in state education funding. For POWER, a defense of hold harmful was not only a policy position, but it was also a defense of the racial school funding status quo; it meant perpetuating racial inequity in school funding.

Second is the "color-blind managerialism" project (Turner 2020:24). Advocates of this approach "articulate a commitment to (racial) equity . . . [but] there is no attention to power or structural racism in this conception of equality; social change is accomplished through managerial mechanisms" (Turner 2020:25). This typifies the work of the ed associations (also referred to as "unions" or "membership-driven organizations") within PA Schools Work. For them, eliminating hold harmful was not only too radical and too unrealistic, but it was also *unnecessary* because they didn't view the unequal distribution of school funding as an example of structural racism writ large. They favored increased funding that would, as they saw it, equally benefit *all* their member districts.

The third grouping—those in the middle (i.e., the more progressive policy advocacy organizations)—did a little of both. They tried to move the needle of school funding toward racial equity by proposing accelerated funding for the neediest school districts, while also calling for increases to the state education budget, understanding that a fairer distribution of a too-small pie is rendered useless. They knew and agreed with the critiques of colorblindness, but also exercised colorblindness for political reasons. Here I offer another type of racial project—*the strategic colorblind racial justice project*. Adherents of this type of racial project are racially conscious and articulate racial justice as a goal, but their methods strategically employ colorblindness to play to the sensibilities of lawmakers and the unions. Donna Cooper, who spoke of the "curse of a child's zip code" is an example of this.

Although the "middle" groups tried to stand their ground by introducing equity proposals, the ed associations stymied these attempts each step of the way. Under the banner of being "unrealistic" or "not politically viable," the ed associations were unwilling to support any proposal that made a substantive step toward equity, much less the elimination of hold harmful. The construction of policy proposals was overdetermined by the actions of union leaders just as "cerebral commitments to racial justice [are often] undermined by nonblack people's visceral commitment to order" (Shange 2019:78). The white-led unions "talked the talk" of *equity* but didn't even "walk the walk" of *adequacy*. Instead, they were content with continual small increases. Their call to provide an adequate education for *all* Pennsylvania students, consistently displaced the issue of racial equity in school funding to the detriment of *Black and Latine* students, demonstrating how the use of inclusive language like *all*, and its concomitant "inclusive" tactics, can undermine equity. They willfully neglected the school funding conditions of Black and Latine students by stymieing substantive proposals to advance racial equity in school funding.

## PERSISTENT INEQUITIES

Exposing the underbelly of adequacy discourses has become even more urgent as recent quantitative data analyses have found that racial inequities in school funding will continue in perpetuity if the state legislature fails to address the maldistribution of funding. The notion that increasing the state education budget would benefit *all* districts, but abolishing hold harmful "takes from the hungry to give to the starving"—a position taken by many members of CFEF—is a spurious claim. While it was true that all districts would see their budgets increase if more money were put into the education budget, putting in more money while retaining a policy of hold harmful guarantees that racial disparities in school funding would continue *in perpetuity*.

David Mosenkis (2020) came to this conclusion when he calculated the change in school funding inequity in Pennsylvania, by race, over a period of four years (2016–2020). His line graph shows that despite regular increases to the state education budget during Governor Wolf's tenure ($159 million for 2015–2016; $213 million for 2016–2017; $100 million for 2017–2018 and 2018–2019; and $160 million for 2019–2020), the school funding gap in state aid between the whitest school districts and the least white districts actually *grew* (figure 7). In 2016–2017, the whitest school districts (represented in light gray by the highest line) received $1,934 more per pupil than their fair share (i.e., if all the money were run through the fair funding formula); in 2019–2020, that figure *increased* to $2,234 more per pupil than their fair allotment. Conversely, in 2016–2017, the least white school districts (represented by the darkest gray and lowest line) received $1,912 less than their fair

*Figure 7.* Growing inequities over time. This line graph shows the change in school funding inequities over time between districts with different percentages of white students. Produced by David Mosenkis in 2020.

share; in 2019–2020, they received $2,240 *less* than what they should have received. The school funding gap between the whitest and least white districts was $3,846 in 2016–2017; it grew to $4,474 in 2019–2020.

Zooming into a district-level view, the bar graph in figure 8 (Mosenkis 2020) shows the compounding effects on the School District of Philadelphia, which educates 12 percent of the state's students. In 2015–2016, Philly students were shortchanged $320 million. That number grew to $402 million by 2020–2021. Other school districts in Pennsylvania that serve some of the highest percentages of students of color also experienced rising school funding inequities, including York, Allentown, Harrisburg, Pottstown, and Norristown. A 2020 report by Matthew Kelly, a professor at Penn State University, similarly concluded that inequities in school funding are growing in Pennsylvania. According to a front-page article in *The Inquirer* (October 27, 2020) that featured Kelly's analysis, "Black and Latino students are particularly shortchanged . . . [with] more than 80 percent attend[ing] school districts that would receive more money if the formula were applied fully" (Hanna and Fernandez 2020).

An exclusive focus on increasing the state education budget has widened the racial school funding gap in state aid. These annual incremental increases have exacerbated inequities because they do not

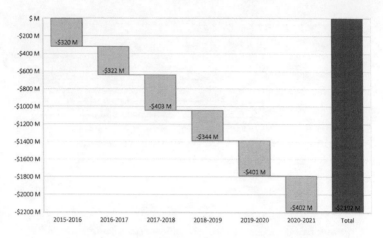

*Figure 8.* School District of Philadelphia funding shortfalls. This bar graph shows the cumulative effect of preserving hold harmful on the School District of Philadelphia. Produced by David Mosenkis in 2020.

fundamentally change the way funding is *distributed*. Even though increases to the education budget also increases the share of funding that goes through the fair funding formula, the policy of hold harmful has ensured that inequities will continue in perpetuity. The idea that increasing state funding will eventually lead to racially fair funding is a common misconception. When David explains his findings of persistent inequalities, he often likes to emphasize this point: we will *never* reach equity by simply putting more money into the current funding structure; racial inequity is getting *worse*, not better.

To those unfamiliar with the minutiae of school funding (including myself before this project), the call to increase funding and provide students with an adequate education appears to be a message that we can and should all get behind. It seems to telegraph improved school funding conditions for *all*. But for majority-minority school districts, that was simply not the case. Though the message of increased funding was conveyed as a universal "win," in actuality, it gave the whitest school districts the greatest comparative advantage. Tinkering toward adequacy in the form of small increases to the education budget has worsened the problem of racial inequity in school funding.

## THE "EXPERTS" PUSH FOR ADEQUACY OVER EQUITY

By fall 2017, the "straight up conflict" among members of CFEF was unavoidable. From the beginning, one of Sundrop Carter's frustrations with the campaign was its promotion of policy experts as CFEF's leaders. These policy experts consistently displaced the issue of racial equity in school funding and foregrounded adequacy instead. She said:

> If you start from the perspective that the experts, and the people who lead are policy people, versus starting from the perspective that . . . the experts are parents and students and teachers, you end up with two different things. And this campaign [CFEF] from the very, very beginning, has started from the [perspective that the] people who are experts are the lawyers, and the policy [people], and the lobbyists, so there's no campaign because they view [the] community as props. It's, "We're going to hold a rally. Can you turn out 20 people?" We've never done that because I don't hand community members out. It's not our job to convince people to take a half day off work to show their face, like, "Look, we've got Brown and Black faces behind us. We're an inclusive thing."

The organizing groups within the campaign felt like they had no real power because "the lawyers, and the policy [people], and the lobbyists" were set up as the experts. In contrast, Carter felt that parents, students, teachers, and Brown and Black folks were the real experts. But instead, they were used as "props" to provide a good photo op—to show "We're an inclusive thing." POWER and PICC felt silenced on substantive issues like the campaign's goals. Their contributions were pigeonholed into turning out people of color for rallies.

CFEF's leadership reflected the campaign's framing of policy people and lobbyists as experts. The chair of the campaign was Joan Benso, a white woman who was, at the time, executive director of Pennsylvania Partnerships for Children (PPC was the organization that only began to mention race on its website after the 2020 uprisings protesting state violence against Black people). PPC is arguably the most politically connected non-union organization within the campaign. Benso was selected to chair the campaign because of her political connections in Harrisburg.

In Benso's role as chair, the campaign centered issues that only policy wonks could engage in, which alienated organizations like PICC and POWER. As one participant explained:

> The campaign's work, because she was the campaign chair, was not really like advancing the interest of communities of color, that people who were representing organizations of color were having difficulty doing their work because there was nothing in the campaign's message that resonated with people, that people didn't feel like they were included in the process.

For comparison's sake, POWER entered the school funding arena *because* communities of color lifted up the issue as one that deeply impacted them. Fair funding emerged organically at the grassroots level. But in her leadership role, Benso managed to create a campaign for *fair* education funding that failed to resonate with communities of color who were most directly impacted by this issue and failed to include mobilization groups. POWER and PICC felt that members of the campaign were unresponsive to their appeals to center the issue of racial equity.

In a last-ditch effort to work out these differences and keep the coalition together, Reverend Greg Holston, then-executive director of POWER, proposed an anti-racism workshop. The two-day workshop took place in Harrisburg in early winter 2017. It was intended to incorporate racial equity into the campaign's goals, address microaggressions experienced by people of color within the campaign and create a new leadership structure.

During the anti-racism workshop, there were red flags that the coalition was tearing at its seams. Organizations like PICC and POWER requested a change in the composition of the executive committee. They wanted to be at the table when consequential decisions concerning the campaign were made. But throughout their time together, people of color within the campaign and leaders of organizations that represented communities of color perceived an unwillingness on the part of CFEF leadership to acknowledge the issues they brought forth. They aired these grievances during the workshop, but to no avail.

Sidelining racial equity is practiced by some of the most respectable people. Benso, around the time of her retirement, received the 2018 William Howard Day Award for a lifetime dedicated to "improving the health, education and well-being of the commonwealth's children" (Pennsylvania School Boards Association 2018). Likewise, representatives of the unions are respected for their work in championing education causes. Though facilitators of the anti-racism workshop did their best to highlight marginalized perspectives, allow grievances to be aired, compile feedback, and set concrete action steps to center the work of racial equity, these respectable education leaders respectfully stuck to their guns. As one member of CFEF informed me, "There were some within the campaign who were not happy at the idea of doing an anti-racism training to begin with because they did not see the work of the campaign to be anti-racism. They were interested in pushing for more funding for their constituents." To the unions, anti-racism training was not only so far removed from what the campaign was about, it was an impediment that diverted important resources and human capital to a nonissue. The unions "did not see the work of the campaign to be anti-racism"; they saw it as a "budget fight," as Carter said earlier. To them, all the talk about race was a distraction from the real work at hand—getting more money for their constituents.

When I interviewed Reynelle Staley, then-policy director of the Education Law Center-PA (ELC), she explained why adequacy was a much easier sell to the ed associations. Staley is at once erudite but approachable, complex but clear, serious but humorous. We immediately bonded over our shared New York upbringing—she Harlem, me Flushing. As one of the few Black women in CFEF, she had to navigate her personal views and her role in the white-dominant space of the campaign. Staley explained to me how the organizational structure of the ed associations shaped their advocacy platform.

> Many of them are membership organizations [and] have members from all across the state. So they're focused on ensuring that every district in Pennsylvania gets more money. So more funding or adequate funding is a priority. I think for me, pursuing ELC's mission means trying to highlight the equity issues.

Ed associations "have members from all across the state," and because a very high percentage of these districts are small, predominantly white districts, these districts' interests are also disproportionately represented within the professional associations. Moreover, because membership-driven organizations feel responsible for ensuring that "every district in Pennsylvania gets more money," they only support measures to increase funding, even if this has shown to widen the racial school funding gap. From the vantage point of the ed associations, adequacy was uncontroversial; it didn't pit member districts, or school boards, or teachers against one another, the way equity proposals (like the elimination of hold harmful) did—a perspective that Staley challenged, both in her role as policy director of ELC charged with "highlight[ing] the equity issues," and personally.

During our interview I asked, "Do you have a viewpoint, a personal viewpoint that's different from your role as policy director?" Staley answered, "I personally find the view that there will be some communities that are harmed by changing the system to dismiss the fact that there are communities that are currently being harmed by the current system." Again and again, the ed associations failed to recognize the harm that their position inflicted on majority-Black-and-Brown districts. Under the facade of a colorblind approach to school funding that putatively benefited all districts, they continued to channel their resources and energy into protecting white-district interests by thwarting equity proposals. To the ed associations, adequacy was a win-win (never mind the Black and Latine students who suffer from this policy—they're used to it). Already disgruntled by the fact that they were forced to participate in an anti-racism workshop they didn't believe in, when the ed associations saw an opportunity to recenter the issue of adequate funding by ousting POWER, they took it.

## THE STRAW THAT BROKE THE CAMPAIGN'S BACK

The straw that broke CFEF's back was POWER's nascent public stance in pushing for all the money to go through the fair funding formula. Staley described the inner workings of the campaign in the following way:

One of the sources of contention between POWER and the old campaign was the fact that they were pushing for all the money through the formula and doing that in a vocal way, which the ed associations particularly felt was undermining their relationship with Republican legislators whose districts would lose if that were the case. And they didn't want it to be the campaign's position or to be associated with a campaign that had members pushing for all the money through the formula.

Republican legislators voted in favor of the fair funding formula in 2016 with the understanding that the formula would only be applied to new money. The ed associations in CFEF were concerned that POWER's new position on school funding changed the terms of agreement between them and state politicians. Being in a campaign with POWER "was undermining their relationship with Republican legislators whose districts would lose" if all the money were driven through the formula. The ed associations were concerned that their credibility would be shot by appearing to be allies with POWER—guilt by association.

Shortly after the anti-racism workshop took place, things came to a boiling point. There were a series of conference calls in quick succession. One noteworthy call involved a subset of campaign members who were supposed to develop an equity platform to provide an alternative to the position of eliminating hold harmful and putting all the money through the formula. This was seen as a more middle-ground approach. The proposal would prioritize districts with greatest financial need and was referred to in many ways, including as an "emergency fix," "equity supplement," "accelerated funding," and "hardship addendum." According to one person's recollection of the event, the organizations represented on the equity call included POWER, PILC, PCCY, ELC, PPC, Allies for Children, as well as the ed associations—PASBO, PASA, PSEA, and PSBA. Since many of the organizations felt that POWER's position on school funding "was not viable . . . as a middle ground, there was discussion about some sort of acceleration funding that would go to underfunded districts," the participant noted.

Rev. Holston (POWER) and Michael Churchill (PILC) developed a proposal in which 30 percent of the state's basic education funding would be set aside for underfunded districts, with the rest of the BEF budget going to the other districts. While this proposal did not undo the policy of hold harmful, it was an attempt to move toward leveling the playing field. The participant viscerally remembered the opposition that ensued.

> The school business officials organization [PASBO] was, like, completely opposed to the idea of it being anything more than 10 percent. And there was like a back and forth. . . . I was in between meetings and being on my cell phone and just like hearing people yelling while there's like construction noise in the background. So people are yelling and then people are like, "I'm just going to hang up."

PASBO thus defanged the equity supplement proposal by blocking "anything more than 10 percent" of the education budget. Given the ed associations' fervent opposition to the equity proposals, one wonders if their participation in this subgroup was a means of protecting their own interests and ensuring that any equity proposal endorsed by the campaign would be more symbolic than substantive.

The last nail in the CFEF coffin was the "infamous conference call," as Carter characterized it. Although it was a year and a half between when the call took place and when I interviewed people about it, the people I spoke with remembered the event with striking detail because of the dramatic fashion in which POWER, one of only two Black-led organizations in the campaign, was forced to leave. Carter referred to the event as "a really sad story," as well as "the perfect case study of why white-led campaigns result in bad decisions, and that actually taking racial justice seriously results in better decision-making."

It began with a roll call in which organizations made their position clear: stop talking about race. Rev. Holston recalled the day with a mix of sadness and astonishment. Publicly, he calls to mind a Black leader from the civil rights era. The cadence of his speeches work toward a crescendo infused with moral conviction. One of my students who heard him speak said, "It gave me chills." Interpersonally, he comes across as soft-spoken and deeply contemplative. He wears a furrowed brow when people aren't looking, lost in his thoughts, and carrying the weight of the world on his shoulders. Recalling the infamous conference call, he said, "The coalition broke up specifically over the issue of race, as POWER kept saying, 'We have to lift up the issue of racial justice and expect that our strategies will do that.' They came back and said, 'No, we don't have the bandwidth to talk about race.'" Lingering on these words and clearly troubled, he said, "I'll never forget that statement: 'We don't have the bandwidth to talk about race.'" Carter also looked back on the event with disbelief: "I've been an organizer for a long time. I've been white my whole life, and it was literally the first time where I heard a series of white people, literally, say the words, 'Racial justice is a distraction. I think we should move on.'" The idea that race was a "distraction" was not an isolated perspective.

One by one, fifteen or so organizations repeated some version of this on the call, which my interviewees recalled in the following ways: "I think racial justice is a distraction from fighting for fair funding," "All of these conversations about racial justice is a distraction from our fight to get more funding for schools," and "I've decided I no longer want to be part of this campaign." Analyzing the event in hindsight, one person said, "Clearly there was a call between that one where everyone hung up and the subsequent campaign call where all of the ed associations, PPC, [and] PCCY had made a pact that they were all going to leave the campaign." Carter noted the irony of this coordinated effort since they had devalued the work of organizing for so long:

> They clearly had organized themselves after dissing organizing for two years. They then organized themselves to do an action on this conference call. . . . They called on each other, so they were like, "I think this is a distraction. I think racial justice is a distraction. I think we need to really move on and focus on the real problem, which is the budget fight. Bob, do you want to go next?"

The coordinated effort was described as "isolating," "backing [Rev. Holston] into a corner," "destroy[ing] Rev. Holston's credibility," and quite simply "unacceptable behavior." While one person disputed the characterization of this event as an "action," what went down is widely agreed upon: the leaders of the ed associations, along with PPC and PCCY, had agreed beforehand to dismantle the campaign by having a critical mass of members leave, and one by one, they censured POWER's position on racial justice.

At the end of the roll call, there was a long moment of silence. Carter punctured the silence by reading a quote from Dr. King's *Letter from a Birmingham Jail*. She told me, it's "the most confrontational I've been." With her heart beating through her chest, she prefaced the quote by saying: "I'm just going to read you a quote that I feel helps guide my work, when I think about my work and doing this." The quote from Dr. King reads in the following way:

> The Negro's great stumbling block in his stride toward freedom is not the White Citizen's Counciler or the Ku Klux Klanner, but the white *moderate* who is more devoted to "order" than to justice; who prefers a negative peace which is the absence of tension to a positive peace which is the presence of justice; who constantly says: "I agree with you in the goal you seek, but I cannot agree with your methods of direct action"; who paternalistically believes he can set the timetable for another man's freedom; who lives by a mythical concept of time and who constantly advises the Negro to wait for a "more convenient season." Shallow understanding from people of good will is more frustrating than absolute misunderstanding from people of ill will. Lukewarm acceptance is much more bewildering than outright rejection. (King 1963)

All the people I spoke with about the infamous conference call used the word "dramatic" to characterize Carter's speech.

Interestingly, though Dr. King's original quote referred to "white moderates," Carter herself and others recounted the event by referring to *white liberals*. It's uncertain whether Carter substituted *white liberal* for *white moderate* during the speech. But since many of the groups and individuals she criticized can be described more accurately as liberals, they remembered *white liberals* as the target of her criticism.

As Carter thought back to that day, she said, "the biggest hurdle in the fight for racial justice . . . [is] white liberals who say, 'Liberation should only come when it's convenient for me.'" Reenacting what happened after the speech, she said: "You just did this. You basically just said, 'We're going to decide when people of color get access to justice, and it's not convenient for me right now, so you all can wait.'" As frustrated as Carter was at their obstruction of racial justice, she also wanted to call out their unwillingness to be accountable for their actions, stating, "If that's the kind of campaign you want, then fine, but let's just be clear." The infamous conference call was especially disappointing to Carter and Rev. Holston because it came on the heels of the anti-racism workshop. Under the justification of needing to focus the work of the campaign, to avoid distractions, and to push for more funding for *all* school districts, CFEF leadership and the ed associations displaced the issue of racial equity. Carter's speech cut to the heart of how white liberalism upholds unequal systems of school funding. Racial equity in school funding is so hard to achieve because white liberal advocates bury the issue.

As it turned out, these groups would continue to wrestle with clarifying the goals of the next campaign, and especially the role that racial equity played (or didn't play) in that process. As for the Campaign for Fair Education Funding, the infamous conference call marked the final chapter of the campaign. Even as many members of the old campaign were reconstituted into a new campaign, POWER branched out to start its own education campaign that focused on dismantling structural racism in Pennsylvania's school funding system.

## "WHEN YOU DISBAND, YOU NEED TO REBRAND"

By the summer of 2018, CFEF had been dismantled, but nearly all its member organizations joined the new PA Schools Work campaign, with the notable exception of POWER. During a conversation I had with a member of PA Schools Work, she expressed genuine confusion about how the campaign could fail to mention race when talking about issues of fair funding. She said it was a recurring "tension" for her. After she briefly recounted the story of how CFEF ended and PA Schools Work began, she wryly stated, "When you disband, you need to rebrand."

Much of the rebranding was cosmetic. While there was a new website along with new language and a new design, the espoused mission of PA Schools Work was strikingly similar to the old campaign. CFEF's mission was to "ensure that Pennsylvania adopts and maintains an adequate and equitable system of funding public education" (Public Interest Law Center n.d.). PA Schools Work stated that it was "fighting for equitable, adequate funding necessary to support educational excellence" (PA Schools Work n.d.). Both campaigns articulated a commitment to adequate and equitable funding, even though both campaigns emphasized adequacy more than equity.

It is notable that even when the PA Schools Work website mentioned equity, it did not explicitly mention *racial* equity. Instead, it used the zip code trope (i.e., "a zip code should not determine a child's future"), stating, "Every child, regardless of zip code, deserves access to a full curriculum, art and music classes, technical opportunities and a safe, clean, stable environment." While a child's zip code is closely correlated to their access to a quality public school, where Black and Brown children live is not random, but rather the effect of de jure and de facto racism in housing and employment (Massey 1990; Rothstein 2017; Taylor 2019). But by mentioning zip code, the campaign was able to take a rhetorical stance on the issue of equity, while avoiding any mention of race.

One of the most salient examples of PA Schools Work's emphasis of adequacy over equity was a public debate between the two campaigns that played out on the pages of *The Delaware County Daily Times*. In February 2019, the editorial board published a piece on school funding that confused the work of the two campaigns. Although it mentioned how PA Schools Work convened a highly successful summit that brought together Delaware County superintendents, principals, students, families, and residents, the editorial board took on *POWER's* position on school funding, stating:

> The most direct route to rectifying the inequities in Pennsylvania's education funding lies in the Legislature, and having them do something they should have done when they enacted the Fair Funding Formula back in 2015. The formula should be applied to all education funding, not just new revenue, which currently limits it to just 10 percent of state education funding. (*Delco Times* Editorial Board 2019)

The editorial board's confusion was understandable since the vast majority of people have not been indoctrinated into the vagaries of school funding politics. To the editorial board, both campaigns used the term "fair funding," and both were trying to improve conditions for schools across the state. The subsequent responses to the editorial piece, first by Susan Spicka, of Education Voters of PA (one of the main organizations in PA Schools Work), then by David Mosenkis, of POWER, elucidated their respective stances.

In a *Letter to the Editor*, published a few days after the editorial board's piece, Spicka wrote that the board was:

> spot-on . . . until its suggested solution to immediately redistrib-
> ute all state basic education funding through the state's new school
> funding formula. That "solution" would require a massive redis-
> tribution of existing dollars, slashing hundreds of millions of dol-
> lars from 357 school districts that educate nearly 813,000 students
> statewide. . . . The bottom line is that Pennsylvania's public schools
> need more state funding, period. Shrinking slices of a pie that's too
> small to make bigger slices for others simply redistributes the pain.
> The only solution is growing the pie, increasing state funding so all
> students in every school district get the resources they need. Aside
> from the policy flaws in your editorial's "solution," it's simply not
> politically viable. Can we expect the legislators who represent 357
> of the state's 500 school districts to stand for such dramatic cuts to
> their own schools? (Spicka 2019)

Spicka, who is white, is seen as one of the more progressive members within the campaign, and yet she reinforced the narrative that "the only solution is growing the pie"—a "solution" that has *widened* racial inequities in school funding. She rejected "massive redistribution of existing dollars" on the basis that 357 out of 500 school districts would have their budgets slashed. She added that it's "not politically viable" to expect that legislators would "stand for such dramatic cuts to their own schools."

Instead of using their advocacy position to reframe legislators' and the public's understanding of "fair funding" and to highlight *racial* ineq-uity, Spicka echoed a well-worn argument in the state legislature: that too many *districts* would suffer because of redistribution—a strategy that prioritizes number of districts over number of *students*. While this strategy was most vigorously advanced by the ed associations, even organizations like Ed Voters endorsed it. By promoting the mindset that the number of *districts* mattered more than the number of *students*, whiter districts (that are more numerous but have fewer students) were prioritized over majority-minority school districts (that have fewer districts but educate more students).

Five days after the *Letter to the Editor* was published, David Mosenkis wrote a guest column, addressing Spicka's points. He lauded the editorial board for their bold endorsement of putting all the money through the fair funding formula and challenged Spicka's logic.

> This commonsense suggestion [of putting all the money through the formula] is simple, fair and politically achievable. It is also essential in order to eliminate the systemic racial bias that for decades has favored whiter districts over comparable districts with more students of color. . . . Critics of 100 percent fair funding, like Education Voters of PA's Susan Spicka in her recently published letter, like to count up the number of districts that would get less funding if all the funds were distributed fairly. They regularly fail to mention that a shift to fair funding would increase funding for the majority of students and the majority of state legislators. It is a false choice to frame funding policy as a choice between increased funding and fair distribution. Pennsylvania sorely needs both. . . . When we have both equitable distribution and increases in funding, fewer districts will face a decrease and more districts will receive truly adequate funding. While reasonable people can disagree over what the total education budget should be, do we really need to argue whether to distribute funding using a proven discriminatory way instead of a universally acclaimed fair formula? (Mosenkis 2019)

In contrast to Spicka's position—increasing state funding for every school district—David argued that choosing between equitable and adequate funding was a "false choice" as "Pennsylvania sorely needs both" (Mosenkis 2019). PA Schools Work was concerned about poor white rural districts that would lose money if the entire education budget was run through the formula, but as David explained, if you also pair this with an increase in the education budget, "fewer districts will face a decrease and more districts [that serve majority-minority students and have been historically underfunded] will receive truly adequate funding" (Mosenkis 2019).

In short, while POWER was willing to endorse putting 100 percent of the money through the fair funding formula *and* an increase in the state education budget, PA Schools Work was not. People within PA Schools Work have criticized POWER's position in advocating for 100 percent as a tactic that "takes from the hungry to give to the starving" because it "simply redistributes the pain." But POWER did not oppose increased state funding. In fact, I have never met a school funding advocate who did. However, POWER felt an urgency to foreground the racial inequities in how the money was distributed, especially since so few groups drew attention to this. POWER's problem with PA Schools Work was that their advocacy for increasing state funding displaced the issue of racial equity.

As Spicka made clear in her piece, an endorsement of 100 percent fair funding was seen as "not politically viable." While demands and campaigns should be achievable, freedom dreams should not be limited by what is immediately politically achievable since real change requires nothing less than making the impossible possible. In Savannah Shange's (2019:21) analysis of the Movement for Black Lives' song-chant, she says, "*I believe that we will win* is an abolitionist mantra that conjures a course to freedom." *I believe that we will win* is a "ritual practice of internalizing the necessity to do the impossible." Internalizing the necessity to do the impossible means being unwilling to settle for *a little less inequity*. As Ella Baker, renowned civil rights activist, poignantly teaches us, "the reduction of injustice is not the same as freedom."

## POWER'S FIGHT FOR 100 PERCENT FULL AND FAIR FUNDING

Demanding the impossible was hard and arduous work. POWER's campaign provides an alternative example of what organizers do when they are unwilling to settle for political viability. This inside look at POWER's strategies and its internal debates over tactics demonstrates what racial justice–oriented organizers were willing to compromise on, and what constituted giving away the store. While the path to justice was long and winding, POWER's organizing work illustrates how it was fueled by joy and camaraderie.

In March 2019, House Bill 961 was introduced by Representative Christopher Rabb, who was elected to the Pennsylvania General Assembly in 2017. The bill "would require 100 percent of state funds for public schools immediately be distributed through the fair funding formula" (Pennsylvania House Democrats 2019). Affectionately known as "Rep Rabb," he has earned a reputation for championing progressive causes including calling for state-level reparations for slavery, 100 percent renewable energy goals, and a clean-slate bill that would limit access to the criminal records of formerly incarcerated people. As a member of the Black Caucus, he and other Black state legislators successfully pushed through a suite of police reform bills in June 2020, buoyed by increased public attention to police brutality. Rep Rabb is well suited for a position in elected office—amiable, knowledgeable about policies, and comfortable with attention. After my students and I met him in his district office, one of them said unironically, "That guy is cool." Rep Rabb collaborated with POWER to draft HB 961.

During a Zoom meeting, Nathan Sooy, a white POWER staff member who organizes in central PA, explained to the education team the purpose of HB 961. Sporting his usual sartorial choice—a button-down shirt with suspenders—Sooy told the group:

> [HB 961] allowed us to expose structural racism and use this situation to further expose the inequity that already exists in the system. You make a demand not because you think you're going to win it immediately, but to show everyone that you're right. As you continue to agitate and organize around it, things have to really change in terms of structures of who has power and who doesn't. HB 961 wasn't a lobby campaign; it was a campaign to expose structural racism.

According to Sooy, the bill was intended "to expose structural racism" and to show "the inequity that already exists in the system." In that sense, POWER's leaders knew that it wasn't something they were going to win immediately. Instead, it was a way to "show everyone that you're right." For all of POWER's campaigns—Live Free, Economic Dignity, and Fair Funding—staff tell volunteers that the underlying goal is "to build power" and strengthen the organizing base. By doing so, you begin to "change . . . who has power and who doesn't."

Notably, Rep Rabb's bill only calls for redistributing existing funds and *not* for increasing the state education budget. While this seems to contradict David's position expressed in the op-ed, he chimed in shortly after Sooy spoke to explain why the bill only focused on redistribution. David said that after they approached Rep Rabb to craft HB 961, "we talked some strategy and some tactics." He said that POWER understands that

> the state doesn't put [in] enough money and it's divided up in unfair ways and disproportionately benefits white students and underfunds students of color. But we decided at POWER and with Rep Rabb that we wanted to focus on that inequity piece. There are a lot of other advocates who are focusing on increasing [the budget] already, but it's not sufficient for us, as people of faith, to say we want to increase everything for everyone, but sustain the inequalities. We said we would focus on the disparities.

As an interfaith organization that sees racial injustice as a moral problem, POWER's position in calling out racial inequity was a moral imperative. While other groups took the path of lesser resistance by advocating for increasing the state education budget, David drew a line in the sand stating, "it's not sufficient for us, as people of faith, to say we want to increase everything for everyone, but sustain the inequalities." As David would later discover through data analysis, "increas[ing] everything for everyone" not only sustained the inequalities, but it also *increased* the disparities. POWER's goals were not limited to what was politically viable, but its position on school funding did serve a practical purpose: to rally its members and "to build power."

Calling for 100 percent of the money to go through the fair funding formula, immediately, was a "clean, clear message" that POWER supporters could easily understand and get behind, as Reynelle Staley, of ELC, told me. This idea was demonstrated during one of POWER's mini retreats when the education team discussed the advantages and disadvantages of endorsing a more moderate approach to school funding. While POWER fully endorsed Rep Rabb's bill, it was also entertaining the idea of lending more support to similar bills that took a more incremental approach, for example, reaching 100 percent over the course of five years.

POWER members who argued for supporting a phase-in approach said that it would increase the number of sponsors of other similar bills, citing that there were state legislators who agreed with the idea of redistribution in principle, but were wary of the upheaval an immediate redistribution would cause to district budgets. They also reasoned that this approach might increase the likelihood that the House education committee would hold a hearing on the issue—the next hurdle in the long road to passing legislation. Having several sponsors on multiple similar bills might create more pressure, some POWER members reasoned.

Others, including myself, argued that POWER's current position—100 percent, now—was a stronger organizing tactic because it was easier for people to understand and rally behind. David chimed in to say, "It's so simple you can chant it. It's easy to say, 'What do we want?' '100 PERCENT!' 'When do we want it?' 'NOW!' It doesn't have the same ring when you say, 'What do we want?' '100 PERCENT!' 'When do we want it?'" Everyone got in on the joke and in unison chanted, "IN FIVE YEARS!" We laughed at the absurdity of that as a protest chant. The debate ended without a definitive answer, but this was an issue that POWER was willing to compromise on since it had previously supported a Senate version of Rep Rabb's House bill that took a more phased-in approach.

Being the lone organization that pushed for a 100 percent approach to fair funding was hard. The work required an unusual level of tenacity and hope—qualities that Rochelle Nichols-Solomon and other POWER organizers exhibited in ample supply. Rochelle wears many hats—two prominent ones being home renovator and community organizer. That night, she had on the community organizer hat. POWER's much-anticipated June 12 (2019) rally at the state capitol turned out one thousand people and was intended to drum up support for HB 961, as well as the phased-in Senate version of the fair funding bill, SB 362.

A week before the rally, Rochelle conscripted me, her daughter, and her daughter's friend to put together 253 "leave-behinds": 203 for each representative in Pennsylvania's lower house, and 50 for each state senator. The leave-behind was a half-sheet cardstock with a cartoon depicting "education apartheid." Two side-by-side images were featured: on the left, a well-funded district with gleaming laptops and smiling white children, and on the right side, an overcrowded classroom with crumbling ceilings, cracked walls, a harried teacher, and distressed Black and Brown children. Explaining the task to us, Rochelle said supporters of HB 961 and SB 362 would receive an elaborate ribbon that they would prominently display during the rally and that this ribbon should be attached to the half-sheet cardstock.

We toiled through the evening in Rochelle's well-styled dining room, which exemplifies her self-proclaimed "avant-garde" sensibilities. As daylight turned to dusk, the dining room was transformed into a makeshift assembly line. I was on pinning duty, Rochelle's daughter stuffed envelopes, and her friend moved between tasks. James, Rochelle's husband, provided an unending supply of sweet treats, wine, and good company, while also serving as quality control. Rochelle popped in from time to time in between her Zoom meetings to playfully chide us for our shoddy work—a ribbon askew here, a crumpled cardstock there. "What happened here?" she queried. "You're not going home until this is all finished!" she threatened. "Trifling" she intoned. We made idle threats to unionize and to initiate a work stoppage, but by the end of the evening we finished pinning seventy-three ribbons onto cardstocks, representing the sixty-three cosponsors for HB 961 and ten senators who supported SB 362. Our small group represented one of many other small groups, laboring together, in joy, to organize a rally of one thousand people.

Brittney Cooper (2018:75) states that joy is essential to "reinvigorating our capacity for a new vision. When we lack joy, we have diminished capacity for self-love and self-valuing and for empathy. If political struggle is exercise for the soul, joy is the endorphin rush such struggles bring." In Rochelle's dining room that evening, the good food and good company, generous hearts and generous spirits, and the wit coupled with merriment demonstrated an important principle that Cooper and adrienne maree brown teach us: the work of organizing and freedom dreaming is pleasure- and joy-filled. It invigorates our capacity to be science fiction writers—"shaping the future we long for and have not experienced" (brown 2019:7). POWER leaders constantly encouraged its staff and volunteers to exercise "prophetic imaginations" and consider a different ontological condition for oppressed peoples. The hard work of getting seventy-three cosponsors (for bills that were considered impossible to pass) was an exercise in keeping elected officials accountable, and an exercise in flexing the prophetic imagination.

Getting that many cosponsors was also a demonstration of POWER's persistence. The rally was one way of applying pressure on state legislators to cosponsor the bill. If they wanted to stand in front of the cameras to tout their support for fair funding, they would be obliged to sign onto the bills first. But POWER organizers also used its congregation-based network to find people who were constituents of targeted legislators. Sometimes getting just one state representative to sign on to the bill required several meetings and a certain unwillingness to hear no. Suffice it to say, getting HB 961 passed was an uphill battle because it required 102 out of 203 votes in the House. Aside from garnering the support of state reps with school districts that would materially benefit from this bill, POWER members also needed to convince legislators with school districts that would *lose* money if HB 961 were passed.[1] Despite the success of the rally and the relatively high number of cosponsors for HB 961, Curt Sonney, the chair of the House Education Committee, refused to give the bill a hearing. Although he agreed to hold a hearing when POWER clergy cornered him in a stairwell during the June 12 rally, he eventually reneged on his promise.

The challenges for POWER included finding new and creative ways to keep the pressure on and to keep people engaged in the work. After the glitz of the rally was over, there was still the behind-the-scenes work of movement-building. As Rochelle often explained, people don't understand how tough it is to transform systems of oppression that have been in place for centuries. A few months after someone participated in a POWER rally, she would sometimes be asked, "Did we get it? Did we get 100 percent fair funding?" Rochelle and fellow organizers work tirelessly to educate people about the structural barriers that make it so difficult to achieve racial equity in school funding, while keeping them hopeful and engaged. She embodies the abolitionist sentiment *I believe that we will win*. It is an organizing truism that the more fundamental the changes, the harder the work. POWER would settle for nothing less than the abolition of the racial school funding gap, which made the work arduous, if not also joy-filled.

## GIVING "LIP SERVICE" TO EQUITY

Even without POWER in the mix, PA Schools Work struggled to get on the same page about what they were fighting for. The ed associations (i.e., PSEA, PSBA, PASA, and PASBO) were against anything that substantively changed the school funding structure; PICC continued to call for centering issues of race in school funding; and progressive-minded groups in the middle, like PCCY (chair of PA Schools Work), ELC, and PILC tried to stitch together the loosening threads of the campaign. Given their divergent positions on school funding, particularly the ed associations' lip service to equity, PA Schools Work predictably stalled out. Although the coalition was built on the idea that different organizations would bring their unique skills to the campaign to successfully effect change, the unfolding story of PA Schools Work suggests that coalitions composed of unlikely bedfellows are ultimately ineffective and a poor use of resources.

Funding sources played a major role in how different organizations engaged in PA Schools Work. Because most of the organizations in the campaign received grant funding from the William Penn Foundation for their participation, some felt financially obligated to stay in the campaign. Sundrop Carter, PICC's leader, was appalled by the ousting of POWER and unhappy that PICC became an *endorsing member*, as opposed to being part of the *governing body* in the campaign. "We have no power," Carter said. "We literally, structurally have no power." And yet leaving the campaign would have meant leaving behind grant money that PICC had already budgeted for.

The ed associations were not financially dependent on the grant because they were mainly funded through membership dues. Their motivation for participating in the campaign was to "get money for their members," as someone in PA Schools Work told me. Instead of being financially obligated by the grant, the ed associations were beholden to the interests of their member districts, teachers, and superintendents, most of whom were benefiting from the racial school funding status quo. The divergent interests of these organizations made for a challenging experience. I spoke with a member of the PA Schools Work campaign and asked questions about her experiences in the campaign.

"So how would you characterize the PA Schools Work campaign?" I asked.

"Um, frustrating," she said, followed by a soft chuckle. It surprised me that she answered with so little hesitation.

Among the frustrations she cited was the Republican-controlled legislature that made it veritably impossible to push through any meaningful changes to school funding, as well as Governor Wolf's disappointingly small "ask" for education funding even though he had won reelection. But the core of her frustration had to do with the dynamics of the campaign itself. She said that the ed associations were "giving lip service to issues of equity," even as they stymied efforts to advance equity in school funding.

> I think there's a whole other element of an issue we talk about out here, about some of the organizations giving lip service to issues of equity, but really only focusing on issues of adequacy of funding . . . even though it's consistently restated as, "Yes, of course, we agree with the equity goals of the campaign," but you know, then when you try to make it tangible, some of these organizations will say "no we can't really support that." So in some sense, it feels like organizations don't have any problem with acknowledging, stating, even forcefully, that Pennsylvania has have- and have-not school districts. But if you make concrete proposals for how the have-nots could get more, they don't seem to get anywhere unless they're universal.

She noted how the ed associations could even "forcefully" acknowledge the problem of inequitable funding by stating that there are "have- and have-not districts." And yet when the more equity-minded organizations in the campaign tried to "make concrete proposals for how the have-nots could get more," they would consistently hit a dead end. The equity proposals "don't seem to get anywhere unless they're universal," which of course negates the equity aspect of the proposal. On paper, PA Schools Work was "fighting for equitable, adequate funding" (PA Schools Work n.d.), but in practice, it only focused on issues of ade-

quacy of funding or increasing funding for all districts because of the
position of the ed associations.

The Equity Collaborative consisted of a subset of leaders from
within PA Schools Work and was intended to keep issues of equity
on the agenda. This smaller group included leaders from PCCY (chair
of the PA Schools Work campaign), as well as ELC, PILC, the Urban
League, and the four professional ed associations. The Equity Collaborative's conference calls were often marked by the ed associations' tacit
opposition in the form of silence or outright rejection of any concrete
proposal. *Forbearance* characterized the rest of the Collaborative.

A few participants retold various examples of these conference
calls, with one participant remembering a particular call with episodic
detail. During that call, Tomea Sippio-Smith, policy director of PCCY,
and one of the few Black women in the campaign, had the unenviable
position of trying to wrangle participants to agree on a proposal to
channel money to the thirty-eight neediest school districts in Pennsylvania. Michael Churchill (PILC), the white, elder statesman with
a steel-trap memory for details, objected to any proposal that would
circumvent the 2016 fair funding formula. He argued that the former
campaign—CFEF—had worked hard to get the fair funding formula
passed and felt that any proposal that bypassed it would destroy the
very thing they fought for. Reynelle Staley, the Harlem-raised policy
director of ELC, also asserted the need for a proposal to be significant
and substantial enough to support equity, insisting that PA Schools
Work should demonstrate a commitment to the equity principle.

But one after another, representatives from the ed associations, all
white men, chimed in, mostly to register their objection. Eric Elliott,
of PSEA, said that a long-term supplement would not be viewed fa-
vorably by his organization. John Callahan, from PSBA said he would
oppose any proposal that championed some districts over others and
that the campaign should advocate for *all* school districts. Jay Himes
(PASBO) took a more conciliatory position and supported a one-time
supplement arguing that until the lawsuit *William Penn School District
v. PA DOE* forced systemic change, this group would have to work
around the fringes.

"Do we do something or nothing?" the participant recalled Himes
asking rhetorically.

Fed up with the idea of "realistic asks" and the calculus of political viability, Churchill suggested not having an "ask" at all. A "realistic ask," as he saw it, was way below what school districts needed to educate its students. Churchill wanted to be in the business of advocating for what districts *actually* needed; not simply accept what the governor and legislators were willing to dole out. Making a "realistic ask" would be "falling into their game." This was essentially a modified version of "don't hate the player, hate the game." A participant recalled how Churchill was "opposed to having a BEF ask."

Every year, this campaign, and the campaigns before it, engaged in a ritual practice of making an "ask" ahead of the governor's budget proposal. The practice was as constant as the ocean tides. Making an "ask" was supposed to push the governor's proposed education budget higher than it would have been. The "ask" also gave campaigns the opportunity to take credit and declare a "win" in the event of a significant increase. A "win" solidified and enlarged the campaign's base of supporters. Churchill's drastic proposal to oppose "a BEF ask" was a sharp break from tradition, intended to highlight the profundity of inequitable funding in Pennsylvania. It was meant to expose the unwillingness of the governor and state legislature to give districts what they actually needed to educate students. In that moment, Churchill suggested that the campaign practice a politics of refusal, reasoning that making a realistic "ask" was "falling into their game."

Audra Simpson (2014) theorizes about the politics of refusal practiced by Kahnawà:ke Mohawks in settler colonial contexts. Simpson says that in sharp contrast to a politics of recognition, which accepts settler colonialism as a fait accompli, refusal calls into question the legitimacy of settler governance and writes a different story—a story of indigenous sovereignty and the unfinished work of settler colonialism. A politics of refusal rejects a "win" that is predicated on existing structures. Churchill proposed practicing a politics of refusal on the premise that a realistic ask didn't even chip away at the problem. But in the end, the coalition's necessity for a "win" was too great. As Shange (2019:158) insightfully instructs, the "'nonprofit industrial complex' . . . is a *libidinal* economy that disciplines the desire for freedom into a quantifiable goal—an endpoint that can be lauded on a successful end-of-year grant report." It "neatens unruly dissent . . . and shoehorns insatiable demands . . . into winnable campaigns" (Shange 2019:158); it transforms what our districts *actually* need into what is a "politically viable" win.

Despite Churchill's impassioned speech, Sippio-Smith moved forward, recapping elements of a proposal she thought the group could reach consensus on—a one-time supplement, distributed through the fair funding formula, and directed toward the neediest school districts. She asked if anyone wanted to add to her understanding, and a short pause followed.

"Got agreement," Churchill said, eager to seal the deal. His quick 180 reflected his willingness to compromise since this proposal not only used the fair funding formula, but also acknowledged that high-needs districts should get additional funding. His reversal also signifies the fine line between a more radical framing of school funding that practices a politics of refusal and irrelevance.

In a *not so fast* moment, John Callahan (PSBA) responded that he obviously didn't agree but would have to deal with it in the next call.

The way in which the ed associations gave "lip service" to equity but stymied concrete proposals was repeated time after time. They actively stewarded discussions toward school funding stasis. Their implacable position was predetermined by the fact that their members, who would lose out if hold harmful was eliminated, paid the bills. Their financial bottom line dictated their ideological bottom line: preservation of the racial school funding status quo. In the end, the coalition's effectiveness was gripped by divergent positions on school funding. Finding agreement on a substantive equity proposal was pie in the sky. So much work resulted in so little change.

### "BABY STEPS"

The ed associations, particularly PSBA in this case, actively worked to maintain the school funding status quo by filibustering any substantive discussion of redistribution, and by paternalistically suggesting that only "baby steps" were possible. In 2015, David Parker, a Pennsylvania state legislator, proposed an amendment to the school code that would have eventually funneled all the money through the fair funding formula.[2] Parker, the former Republican representative from Monroe County, was motivated to change the school funding structure because the local taxes were too high for his constituents, especially for seniors who were on a fixed income. He talked about how "those four groups"—PSBA, PSEA, PASA, and PASBO—actively lobbied representatives to vote against his bill, "and pretty much if they're coming out against it, that's who the other representatives listen to."

Parker recalled a "really frustrating thing during that hearing" (when his bill was discussed). A representative from PSBA "was filibustering and just killing time" by "talking about all these things that we already know." Conveying the paternalistic attitude of the ed associations, he said, "They definitely didn't want any change to the way they were doing the formula. They knew what's best." Parker told the following story that occurred after the hearing:

> I had a Stroudsburg school board member at the hearing with me and he talked to [the PSBA rep] because he was a . . . he's on the school board and this school board guy is supposed to represent school boards. And [the Stroudsburg school board member] just said, "Why are you against us? This is, you know, this is what we need to do." And [the PSBA rep] just said, "Baby steps, we can only take baby steps."

Parker was initially motivated by a concern for seniors in his district who were on fixed incomes and saw their property taxes increase each year because of the state's low share of education aid. He expressed disappointment in only learning about David Mosenkis's findings after he left the state legislature. Although Parker wasn't aware of the findings of racial bias at the time of the hearing, this PSBA rep almost certainly was. This exchange took place in 2015, when POWER and PSBA were both in the Campaign for Fair Education Funding, and David Mosenkis had already testified about racial bias in education funding in November 2014. Although Parker's proposed amendment was not publicized as a way to eliminate racial bias in school funding, this PSBA rep likely knew the effect it would have.

When the PSBA representative placated the Stroudsburg school board member by encouraging him to "take baby steps," it was another way of filibustering racial equity in school funding. It calls to mind Carter's speech during the infamous conference call when she quoted Dr. King's indictment of white moderates (and liberals) for "paternalistically believ[ing] he can set the timetable for another man's freedom"; and for "constantly advis[ing] the Negro to wait for a 'more convenient season.'" Like Rep. Oberlander and other state legislators whose *intention* in supporting hold harmful was to protect "districts including my own," but willfully turned a blind eye to the devastating *effects* of the policy on Black and Brown children, this PSBA representative wanted to protect the interests of PSBA's majority-white membership, with little concern for the effect this had on majority-minority districts.

In the exchange above, "baby steps" was deployed to thwart equity. But I want to reconceptualize that to consider how "baby steps" can signify new growth and possibilities. These new possibilities and collaborations began to emerge as the campaign became less saddled by organizations that only gave "lip service" to equity.

Though PICC was only an endorsing member of the campaign, that didn't stop Sundrop Carter from continuing to try to center race in the work of the campaign. In May 2019, I published an op-ed in *Colorlines* titled, "Why We Can't Afford to Leave Race Out of School Funding Conversations" (Liu 2019). Carter referenced the piece in an email with the subject, "Race and school funding." The body of the email stated:

Dear PA Schools Work,

Happy Friday! I thought many of you would find this piece relevant to our work here in PA: **Why We Can't Afford to Leave Race Out of School Funding Conversations [Op-Ed]. Colorlines.com**

Although this piece is mostly focused on lawyers and legal strategy, I think it applies equally to policy advocacy work, like the work this coalition is engaged in.

- Sundrop

Describing herself as a "broken record," Carter relentlessly called attention to the conspicuous absence of conversations around racial equity in school funding, often in ways that rattled other campaign members.

During a pro forma presentation to the funders, Carter "went rogue," as one person described it. The event was supposed to celebrate the accomplishments of the campaign—"What great work we're doing," etc. Scripted presentations were made by various campaign members, until Carter said something along the lines of, "And they're still not including . . . the mobilization groups and communities of color," as someone recalled.

Frustrated as Carter was by the campaign, she nevertheless found a silver lining: finding like-minded organizations to partner with. Referring to the upside of being a "broken record," she said:

> So I think that's a good thing, because I don't know if we would have ever. . . . It would probably have taken us a little bit longer to figure out how to partner with ELC and [PA] Budget and Policy [Center] if they hadn't approached us because we've been very publicly critical saying, like, "Here are all the gaps. What are y'all going to do about this?" And so they've reached out like, "Well, let's work together on this."

Carter described groups like ELC and PA Budget and Policy Center as being "more aligned politically" with PICC. But because of their roles within the campaign, they were not as vocal as Carter was. Nevertheless, emergent collaborations had formed.

Elizabeth Povinelli (2014) writes about how the possibility of an "otherwise" is built into existing arrangements. Therefore, even when the given order and given arrangement seems hegemonic, there always exists the possibility of derangements and rearrangements. She states:

> *The* plane of existence is not *one* plane of existence. It is always more than one, even as it is becoming hegemonic or maintaining its hegemony. . . . But every arrangement installs its own possible derangements and rearrangements. The otherwise is these immanent derangements and rearrangements. (Povinelli 2014:1)

Though colorblindness and "giving lip service" to equity were hegemonic in the campaign, these emergent collaborations between the mobilization groups and the more progressive child advocacy organizations created the possibility of derangements and rearrangements, of not only allyships, but also of notions of equity.

The possibilities of rearrangements were open and indeterminate. On the one hand, organizations like PCCY, PILC, PA Policy and Budget Center, and ELC saw value in having organizations like PICC and POWER serve as a "left flank to move the legislature to the left," as Staley explained. But they also saw value in having the ed associations, who had political clout, be part of the campaign. Deborah Gordon Klehr, executive director of ELC said that "members within the campaign have strong relationships in Harrisburg with Republicans and Democrats and the governor's office and people in decision-making positions and have been able to, I think, get the message out around adequacy." They were effective in one part of what she believed was a two-part formula: "You have to grow the pie *and* redistribute" (italics mine). As Klehr explained, redistributing a too-small pie does no one any good. But for all the success in getting "the message out around adequacy," the ed associations did not use their political capital to press the issue of equity and actively torpedoed equity proposals. The child advocacy organizations frequently felt caught in the middle and frequently played the part of mediator in maintaining existing arrangements.

Though promoting adequacy was done under the guise of wanting all districts to benefit, white rural districts that have historically received more than their fair share benefited the most. In a panel on abolitionist teaching that included Bettina Love, Gholdy Muhammad, and Dena Simmons, Simmons put things into perspective when she talked about the compassion of Black women, saying, "You're lucky we want equality and not revenge." Advocates of racial equity were not seeking revenge by having white districts experience the pain of underfunding their children. Organizations within PA Schools Work did not endorse 100 percent redistribution because they wanted to protect low-wealth white rural districts. POWER, which *did* call for 100 percent redistribution, *also* supported increased funding so that white rural districts would be spared the pain of draconian cuts that districts like Philadelphia have had to make over the decades. But white-district domination was reified when ed associations vocally endorsed increased funding and consistently opposed equity proposals.

At the end of my interview with Rep. Mike Sturla, who is no stranger to issues of school funding, having served as a member of the BEF Commission, I said, "One last question. Are you familiar with the PA Schools Work campaign and what they do?" "No, I'm not," he answered, without skipping a beat. In our one-hour-long interview, we chatted about POWER and their work with Rep Rabb, but not once did he bring up PA Schools Work because he had no knowledge of the campaign's work. The ed associations had forced the campaign's message to be so watered down, so "realistic" and so "politically viable" that PA Schools Work blended into the everyday political machinations of Harrisburg.

Bettina Love (2019) explained the need to deliberately center issues of race and equity in social movements, including, or perhaps especially, in the most seemingly progressive movements. Referring to the widespread education cuts since the Great Recession of 2011, she noted how the nationwide teacher strikes of 2018 forced many teachers into debt. She states: "I therefore support teacher strikes; however, we need to be critical of strikes that are not centered around issues of equity and race, because history tells us that dark people will always get the short end of the deal" (Love 2019:107). The dynamics that I described in this chapter are precisely what Love warned us against. Through focusing on the issue of *adequacy*, through arguing that race was a "distraction" from the budget fight, through delays of justice, and through encouraging "baby steps," a campaign for "fair" and "equitable" funding wound up undermining racial equity and maintaining the status quo.

The racial school funding gap is historically contingent and dependent on a series of actions and decisions. Displacing racial equity and silencing the voices of people of color are not givens; they are a choice. You could have "white folx bringing dark folx in on all decision-making and dark folx having equal or more weight" (Love 2019:121). The perpetuity of the racial school funding gap is not a given. I end on a more hopeful note in the next and last chapter of the book, showing how things can be different. With several unions pulling out of the campaign, and political winds blowing in favor of a newly formed equity collaborative within PA Schools Work, the fight for racial equity in school funding accelerated and gained traction. This reconfiguration expanded the possibilities for allyship and for centering more substantive proposals that positively impacted majority-minority districts.

CHAPTER SEVEN

# Broadening Our Vision for School Funding

I began this book with remarks from Rich Askey, the president of PSEA, the state's teachers' union. At that time, he proudly proclaimed the "great progress" of the coalition in funding Pennsylvania's schools, despite knowledge of racial disparities and inadequacy of funding. By mid-2020, some members of PA Schools Work, fortified by nationwide protests for racial justice, were calling for more explicit language about the disparate impact of school funding on Black and Brown communities. From PSEA's perspective, the "great progress" of the coalition was receding because of the new attention paid to issues of racial equity. By early to mid-2020, PSEA and PSBA (the school board association that encouraged "baby steps") had had enough. Coinciding with the start of the pandemic and the end of the grant cycle, both organizations pulled out of the campaign.

This final chapter shows what was achieved when racial justice obstructionists left the coalition. These derangements and rearrangements led to centering issues of racial equity in school funding and producing some of the coalition's most substantive wins. I reflect on the challenges that social justice–oriented coalitions, nonprofits, and foundations face in working within the nonprofit industrial complex and call for a clear-eyed vision of freedom that extends beyond grant cycles and "SMART" goals. I also call on us to imagine otherwise school funding systems and offer a reparations-based approach outlined by other scholars. I end with wisdom from my favorite protagonist in the book—Rochelle, who urges us to sustain the struggle through joy and celebration.

## CENTERING RACE IN THE LEVEL UP PROPOSAL

By 2021, with PSEA and PSBA out of the picture, fourteen of the more progressive nonprofit organizations in PA Schools Work[1] created a subgroup of partners that focused on equity. The initiative was called *Level Up* and the goal was to "level up school funding for our most underfunded schools" (Level Up School Funding n.d.a). Unlike the colorblind strategies that dominated the work of the larger coalition, this subgroup, led by the Education Law Center, were more direct about issues of race, stating that the "most underfunded districts serve a disproportionate share of the Commonwealth's students of color, students living in poverty, students with disabilities, and English learners" (Level Up School Funding n.d.a).

Level Up acknowledged that school funding was inadequate *and* inequitable along racial lines. It also acknowledged that only funneling new money through the formula was a problem, stating that "at the current rate of increase in state educational spending, it will take decades or more for the most underfunded districts to reach adequate funding" (Level Up School Funding n.d.b). The initiative, referred to as the "Level Up equity supplement," proposed that at least $100 million of new money be earmarked for one hundred of the most underfunded districts;[2] that the money be distributed through the fair funding formula; and that this funding be included in each district's basic education funding pot, not just a one-time infusion of money.

According to Level Up partners, the beneficiaries of this proposal would be:

- 65 percent of Pennsylvania's Black students
- 58 percent of Pennsylvania's Latine students
- 58 percent of Pennsylvania's students in poverty
- 64 percent of Pennsylvania's English learners
- 35 percent of Pennsylvania's students with disabilities
- 32 percent of Pennsylvania's total student population (Level Up School Funding n.d.b)

These districts significantly overlapped with the districts that POWER had been advocating for, but excluded affluent suburban districts that would have received money if all the basic education funding were distributed through the formula. The analysis for this proposal was conducted by a staff member of PASBO, one of the ed associations. Though PASBO was not formally part of Level Up, it collaborated with PA Budget and Policy Center and Michael Churchill (PILC) to craft a more fine-tuned way of getting additional money to the most struggling districts. Their proposal avoided having some funding unnecessarily funneled to predominantly white wealthy suburban districts, which would have happened if all the money were run through the fair funding formula because of their increased student populations. According to Level Up's analysis, directing money to the one hundred most underfunded districts had a more positive school funding impact on Black and Latine students than running all the money through the fair funding formula.

It should be noted that these kinds of race-based analyses were a hopeful development. Recall David Mosenkis's comment that racial biases in Pennsylvania state aid were "always there" and "anybody could've, if they dug into the numbers, found this pattern of racial bias." But no one did because no one was asking those questions back in 2014. By 2021, Level Up not only asked those questions and conducted those kinds of analyses, but they also put forth proposals that centered the financial needs of majority-minority school districts. To sum up the most positive aspects of the Level Up equity proposal, the money was directed to the students that needed it the most; the methodology for identifying the one hundred districts was transparent (it did not replicate the behind-the-scenes wheeling and dealing of earmarked funding that favored districts with state legislators in positions of senior leadership); and it was more explicit about racial disparities in funding than the coalition had ever been before.

The Level Up initiative was largely successful in securing its funding goals. On June 25, 2021, the state legislature agreed to increase basic education funding by $300 million (Hughes and Couloumbis 2021), to a total of $6.25 billion. But also, because of Level Up's advocacy work, funding was targeted and accelerated toward some of the most underfunded districts. Of the $300 million, $200 million was distributed to all districts through the fair funding formula; the remaining $100 million would also be distributed through the fair funding formula but was reserved for the 100 most underfunded schools (Hughes and Couloumbis 2021).

According to David Mosenkis, who conducted an analysis of the 2021–2022 budget, it resulted in a "modest increase in funding to all the districts POWER cares about." While the budget decreased inequity between the most and least white districts, from $2,263 per student to $1,174 per student, some of this was related to a change in Philadelphia's fair share of formula funding. The real estate market value for Philadelphia (one measure used to calculate each district's fair share) had increased dramatically, therefore lowering Philadelphia's fair share of funding from $1.56 billion to $1.46 billion. Since Philadelphia is the largest school district in Pennsylvania, and certainly the largest school district among majority-minority districts, it had a substantial effect on the overall average in terms of calculating inequity. This gave the appearance that the racial school funding gap was being addressed in a more significant way than it really was.

### "FUCK PRACTICAL"

There is an underlying tension that suffuses the work of organizing and advocacy groups. On the one hand, there is the need for a "win" that will spur change and generate momentum and support. On the other hand, there is recognition that anything easily attainable falls short of what is needed. That tension was conveyed in Level Up's press release, which took credit for the 2021–2022 education budget "win," while also acknowledging that state leaders had not done enough. The press release stated that the equity supplement "is a bright spot in this year's underwhelming budget agreement—a small, but meaningful step in the right direction. It will accelerate funding to some of Pennsylvania's most underserved students, for whom profoundly inadequate resources remain the norm."

POWER also had internal debates about the extent to which they should be practical and support initiatives, like Level Up, that tinkered toward more funding for districts in need, or to hold firm to their position of 100 percent fair and full funding. For some POWER organizers, the stance to abolish racial disparities in school funding was a moral imperative that should not be compromised. For others, refusing to support initiatives that were more in the realm of political possibility made them irrelevant and put them at odds with potential allies.

The governor's 2022–2023 budget proposal brought these issues to the fore. Governor Wolf proposed a historic increase of $1.25 billion in state education aid to the existing $7.1 billion basic education funding budget. Unlike last year, when Wolf suggested putting all the money through the fair funding formula, he "did not repeat his call for allocating all of it through the fair funding formula since that has been a nonstarter with the legislature" (Mezzacappa 2022). Instead, he proposed putting $300 million toward the "Level Up" districts. According to the School District of Philadelphia's analysis, the governor's proposal, if passed, would bring $410 million of new money into Philly schools.[3] Superintendent Hite said it would "significantly improve the District's long-term financial outlook, allowing us to make new investments [that] our students and schools deserve" (Mezzacappa 2022).

I chatted with Rochelle about the dynamic of practicality on the front porch of her daughter's house. I was dropping off a birthday burrito when Rochelle unexpectedly came to the door. In between talking about weekend plans, she told me about POWER's recent debate over whether to support the governor's 2022–2023 budget, which had been shaped by the Level Up proposal.

"I mean, people who think . . . I don't . . ."

Rochelle momentarily struggled to find the words to convey her feelings. But then, evoking her mother—the well-respected Philadelphia activist, Mamie Nichols, who was referred to in an *Inquirer* article as being like a "college professor, but not above using an occasional word that cannot be printed in a family newspaper" (Hollman 1992)—Rochelle quickly landed on, "Fuck practical." With a characteristic tone in Rochelle's voice that can be detected in three generations of Solomons—a voice that I have come to associate with moral clarity and truth telling—she continued, "I'm not concerned about practical . . . strategic is different, but practical, no." The truth teller, we are reminded, "must be willing to put herself at risk before she is able to create a new world in which she can securely exist" (Povinelli 2012:459). While Rochelle was not unequivocally against supporting the governor's budget or the Level Up proposal, this notion of needing to support it because it was "practical" offended her. Centering advocacy and organizing around what's "practical" limits the horizon of what we think Black and Brown children deserve and the value we place on their lives. That is why, even though POWER ultimately supported the governor's budget, its own campaign was organized differently.

"Fuck practical" could have been POWER's campaign slogan. The campaign and the associated bill (HB 961, sponsored by Representative Chris Rabb) proposed that 100 percent of basic education funding should be distributed through the fair funding formula *not* because it was "practical," but because it demonstrated that systemic racism exists in the state's school funding system. The campaign revealed the chasm between a racially fair distribution of funding and what legislators were *willing to do*; it exposed the structural racism that made "allocating all of it through the fair funding formula . . . a *non-starter* with the legislature" (Mezzacappa 2022, italics added). "Fuck practical" pointed to how the core problem wasn't a practical one, it was an ontological one, having to do with the project of race-making and the differential valuing of lives. The campaign demonstrated how the state assigned different values to different children's lives through its distribution of school funding. "Practical" meant accepting that Black and Brown children were less worthy than white children. "Fuck practical" was a rejection of the pervasive paternalistic attitude that asks, "What more do you want?" If "practical" meant working within existing political systems of power and forms of governance, then "fuck practical" was a rejection of the current political order and its forms of governance because "modern governance *is* institutional racism" (Rosa and Díaz 2020:123, italics added).

## THE NONPROFIT INDUSTRIAL COMPLEX AND OTHERWISE COALITIONS

Coalitions are often built around the lowest common denominator—the one thing that all groups can agree on. More often these days, coalitions are also built around grant funding. Both these factors were at play in the formation of Pennsylvania's school funding coalitions. Supported financially through grants, the William Penn Foundation played a significant role in the shape and dynamics of these coalitions, which have spanned over two decades. The foundation was one of the main architects of the more recent coalition, Campaign for Fair Education Funding, which became PA Schools Work when POWER was ousted. The William Penn Foundation put great thought into designing a school funding coalition. They imagined that an effective coalition would be composed of organizing groups that could build grassroots support, ed associations/ unions that had the political clout to push for change, and child advocacy organizations that had policy expertise and the ability to facilitate collaboration. This theory of change seemed to make a lot of good sense. But in reality, members of the coalition not only had different, but divergent approaches to school funding; approaches that were so conflictive that it hindered the work of racial equity. The outcome of these events should prompt us to pause and consider what kinds of coalitions facilitate a radical liberatory imagination and praxis, and particularly, the efficacy of coalitions that are established through foundations.

Designed in large part by the William Penn Foundation, grant funding was predicated on having coalition members work together for a common cause. While it was true that all the organizations shared the "common goal" of securing more education funding from the state, a few organizations, most notably the grassroots groups, did not want additional funding to come at the expense of sidelining issues of racial equity and their demand to redistribute funding. More for *everyone* did not address the problem that majority-minority districts were systemically shortchanged. Sidelining issues of race, however, was precisely what took place in the Campaign for Fair Education Funding, and much of PA Schools Work, until recently with the work of Level Up (the equity-focused subgroup of PA Schools Work). The ed associations, wary of upsetting a school funding status quo that privileged its whiter school districts, made every effort to thwart racial equity proposals put forth by other members of the coalition. They pushed the coalition to do what was "practical" and politically feasible.

With money on the line, organizations that depended on grant funding felt compelled to stay in the arrangement, curtailing their ability to offer more radical proposals. Coalition-building is a staple of organizing work. Grassroots organizers who centered their work on issues of race were not opposed to building coalitions. However, they were opposed to participating in coalitions that required them to be mute on issues of race. What kinds of coalitions and political conjunctures can then lead to liberatory futures?

Ruth Wilson Gilmore's (2017) ruminations on the nonprofit industrial complex and the dangers and opportunities of foundation funding provide insight into this question. With clear analogues to the military and prison industrial complexes, the nonprofit industrial complex is a critique of the enmeshed political relationships between nonprofits, businesses, and foundations such that social justice goals and methods are rigorously managed and curtailed. Gilmore (2017:51) refers to this as the process in which "forms create norms." Grant reports and funding rubrics that dictate "SMART" (i.e., Specific, Measurable, Achievable, Realistic, and Time-bound) goals subdue radical and liberatory social imaginaries in favor of what's practical and politically viable.

The concept of the *otherwise* has been offered to signal emergent political potentialities including new political thoughts and configurations. Elizabeth Povinelli, in her analysis of Foucault, writes that the conditions of the otherwise lie in the radical spaces created for truth telling and performative public worldmaking. This "opens the field of truth and in the process exposes the truth and the subject to a number of permutations whose effects the subject cannot yet know" (Povinelli 2012:459). In other words, the indeterminacy and multiple potentialities of an otherwise are wholly incompatible with grant funding structures and rubrics that require a strong degree of certainty and feasibility. And yet, because photocopies need to be made and the labor of organizers and advocates need to be compensated, grants from funding agencies are still one means in which activists in nonprofit organizations can advance the work of truth telling. Despite the dependency and accommodation of nonprofit organizations to funding agencies, the nonprofit industrial complex "did not destroy the US mid-century freedom movement; activists took down US apartheid in its legal form" (Gilmore 2017:41), thus pointing to the possibilities of the strategic use of grants for "achieving non-reformist reforms on the road to liberation" (Gilmore 2017:41).

Foundations are not one size fits all. Some have funded projects that are stringent critiques of the current order—projects that have sought to materially instantiate an otherwise. In the case of the William Penn Foundation, one person I spoke with recalled an exchange in which a program officer urged members of the coalition to be more vocal about systemic racial inequities in the school funding system. This occurred in the wake of the 2020 uprisings and the nationwide racial reckoning. Though some may automatically dismiss this as empty virtue signaling, it nevertheless provides an opportunity for public worldmaking that transforms current racial hegemonies.

Given that the "the entire landscape of social justice is, or will shortly become, like post-Katrina New Orleans because it has been subject to the same long-term abandonment of infrastructure and other public goods" (Gilmore 2017:47), Gilmore recommends that foundations financially support radical worldmaking ideas, not just isolated projects. Projects are limiting because they tend to require the articulation of short-term goals, and the achievement of these goals presuppose working within, rather than transforming existing political and social arrangements. When foundations focus exclusively on funding projects, it malnourishes the capacity to imagine liberatory long-term goals and alternative political possibilities.

Nonprofits also need to secure short-term wins, not just as proof that they are meeting grant-related benchmarks, but more importantly because mobilizing large groups of people requires energizing supporters through these wins. If the story of PA Schools Work could be characterized as an all-too-ready willingness to accept immaterial short-term wins, then POWER's challenge was to secure short-term wins even as it articulated a more radical long-term goal of eliminating racial bias in school funding. One advocate of PA Schools Work expressed it this way: *How many times can you bring busloads of people to Harrisburg to fight for 100 percent full and fair funding before people get tired?*

Working toward radical long-term goals while securing short-term wins requires nonprofit organizations to rethink their relationship with funding agencies, and to have a clear-eyed vision of their work. Although nonprofits have creatively jerry-rigged funding restrictions and oriented them toward radical possibilities, "they did not fool themselves or others into pretending that winning a loss—sticking a plant on a mound of putrid earth in a poisoned and flooded field—was the moral or material equivalent to winning a win" (Gilmore 2017:48). As for POWER, though it did not yet eradicate racial disparities from state education aid, it reframed public discourse around school funding that had, for many decades, remained obstinately colorblind. POWER's goal of having 100 percent of state aid funneled through the fair funding formula was once considered foolhardy, but it has since moved closer to the realm of political possibility.

If Governor Wolf's support of having all the money run through the formula is any indication, then the increasing acceptance of a radical redistribution of school funding was winning a loss. For years, POWER had worked with the governor's office to garner his support. In June 2021, Wolf commented on the state budget that had been passed and said:

> While there is much to celebrate in this bill, it is disappointing that we could not come together to fully provide for the needs of schools. . . . We need all public education funding to go through the fair funding formula to ensure each school district and each student in our commonwealth are getting the support they need. (Commonwealth of Pennsylvania 2021)

Similarly, Level Up's success in accelerating funding to the one hundred neediest districts was winning a loss. Taking foundation money allows nonprofits to win a loss, but they must maintain the moral clarity that enables them to recognize that this is a far cry from winning a win.

Winning a loss requires strategic thinking. When Rochelle said, "I'm not concerned about practical . . . strategic is different," she was, like Gilmore, encouraging an unflinching vision of freedom work. *Strategic* meant "winning a loss" and keeping the long struggle in mind. As Rochelle said in a text to me, it meant "raising the bar . . . saying what is obvious (systemic racism) . . . and building the outrage and demand for the ongoing fight." *Practical*, however, meant being resigned to the current political order to gain a fake win—a win that perhaps bolsters the standing of a nonprofit but ultimately "takes us nowhere."[4] When putatively social justice nonprofits only do what's "practical," it may be time to close shop.

Foundations have erred in their encouragement to bring unlikely allies together. In Pennsylvania, rather than producing a coalition in which organizations used their comparative strengths to productively advocate for increased resources for the state's most under-resourced districts, the most powerful organizations (i.e., the unions) were unwilling to use their political clout to change the racial school funding status quo. In the process, they also stalled efforts led by racial justice–oriented organizations. Though it is easy to be seduced by the idea of bringing disparate groups together under one banner, Gilmore (2017:51) advises us,

> When it comes to building social movements, organizations are only as good as the united fronts they bring into being. . . . But to create a powerful front, a front with the capacity to change the landscape, it seems that connecting with likely allies would be a better use of time and trouble.

Building coalitions that contribute to social movements entails bringing together organizations that can agree on what "winning a win" looks like, are willing to use their political capital to work toward those long-term goals, are strategic (not "practical") about securing short-term wins, and do not confuse the two. As for foundations that articulate a vision for transforming society, their money would be well spent by financially supporting radical worldmaking ideas, not just isolated projects that neatly adhere to existing rubrics.

## OTHERWISE SCHOOL FUNDING SYSTEMS

I originally imagined that this section would provide policy recommendations based on other more equitable school funding systems (e.g., Baker 2021). But as I looked into other systems for financing schools, it became increasingly clear that there were no "models" for what I hoped for. Even when I narrowed the focus to how state systems fared in terms of the racial school funding gap, some reports would give a state a higher rating, while others gave it a lower rating, depending on the methodology used. The search was akin to looking for a racially just needle in a systemically racist haystack.

Also, the differences among school funding systems were incremental. As I continued writing this book, it also became increasingly clear that the purpose of my work—organizing, researching, and writing—was *not* to emulate something that was incrementally better than what Pennsylvania has now. Indeed, Pennsylvania does not need to look to other states to do that; it has been quite proficient in offering incremental and symbolic changes to the school funding system. The problem is not a lack of technical expertise; it's that white-district domination serves as the "neutral baseline" in matters of school funding. What we need to develop and nurture, then, is not the technical know-how for distributing education aid; it's a radical imagination for making worlds anew—worlds in which whiteness does not serve as the default that is protected at all costs. So instead of focusing on what *other* school funding systems have done, this section is dedicated to thinking of *otherwise* school funding systems.

Worldmaking begins from a place of abundance, not false scarcity. The current school funding system operates on a belief that majority-white districts deserve to have their needs met in excess, while majority-Black-and-Brown districts do not get what they minimally need. We have been conditioned to believe that it is normal for "a small minority of our species [to] hoard the excess of resources, creating a false scarcity and then trying to sell us joy, sell us back to ourselves" (brown 2019:10). Abundant justice means "we can stop competing with each other, demanding scarce justice from our oppressors. That we can instead generate power from the overlapping space of desire and aliveness, tapping into abundance that has enough attention, liberation, and justice for all of us to have plenty" (brown 2019:8).

Abolishing hold harmful was once seen as a pie-in-the-sky demand, but later came to frame much of the debate around Pennsylvania school funding and received (tenuous) verbal support from the governor. This demonstrates the importance of not being constrained by what's "practical." How might organizing from a place of abundant justice, rather than practicality, shape our demands of the state?

While school funding campaigns have demanded justice in one area of school funding (i.e., state education aid), there has been little consideration given to how a posture of abundant justice might call for a broader accounting of the harm that's been done and what reparations in school funding might look like. Preston Green, Bruce Baker, and Joseph Oluwole (2021) have done the most serious writing on this topic. They argue that since present-day school funding disparities can be linked to Jim Crow policies around education and housing, reparations are long overdue.

Green and Baker (2021) propose a four-part reparations framework:

1. Provide a tax rebate to Black homeowners, since Black homeowners are often taxed at a higher millage rate because of the low evaluation of their homes—the result of redlining and other forms of housing segregation.
2. Close the overall racial school funding gap between white and Black students. Increased state education aid should be allocated to fund majority-minority school districts with diminished local taxing capacities.
3. Develop school finance formulas that use race as a weight in determining the distribution of education aid. "Because of governmental policies that created racial isolation and the economic disadvantage that accompanies it, school and district racial composition is an important factor to include in state school finance formulas" (Green and Baker 2021).
4. Eliminate policy mechanisms that lead to racial disparities in school funding. While current school finance policies may be facially race neutral, these so-called neutral policies are lineal heirs of policies that have systematically disenfranchised Black people and have produced similar consequences. Though the proverbial packaging changed, the substance remained the same.

I offer Green and Baker's (2021) reparations framework not as *the* answer to school funding disparities, but as an example of broadening our demands, and as an invitation to think, to organize, and to build movements from a place of abundant justice.

While this example of repair and reparations is oriented toward making demands of the state, there are important ways in which political formations reject an orientation toward the state altogether. Deeply skeptical of the state and exercising a politics of refusal, some call for an opting out of the struggle to "form a more perfect union." Instead, they call for a "rending, not reparations" with the state (Shange 2019:4). Reparations commonly appeal to juridical and legislative modes of redress in which a line of injury is traced between those who should be held accountable and those who were harmed, often in individualistic terms. As critical race theorists and anthropologists of race have ably demonstrated, there are serious limitations to pursuing justice through juridical and legislative means since those very structures are designed to maintain the place of whiteness at the top of the racial hierarchy. Belonging "cannot be reckoned through ever-greater adherence to Western norms of discipline, progress, and respectable citizenship" (Thomas 2022:17). That is not to say that we should throw in the towel in court battles, or give up on keeping elected officials accountable, but knowing these limitations requires us to look beyond the juridical-legislative horizon.

For organizers, this post-Katrina landscape of educational abandonment may yet provide a catalyst for organizing outside the framework of the state, for "crisis, creativity, and care are co-constituting; and . . . attunement to the affective dimensions of experience opens portals to more capacious considerations of the engagements that might arise from overlapping histories of dispossession, and ultimately, to repair" (Thomas 2022:17–18). Insofar as reparations do not presuppose repair with the state, it allows us to expand beyond the idea of repairing existing infrastructures, to jerry-rigging state infrastructures toward freedom, liberation, and sovereignty. Just as people in favelas, shantytowns, slums, and—I might add—urban schools have become adept at creatively repurposing conditions not of their making, so too can school funding organizers jerry-rig state resources in ways that "create new forms of collectivity, and forge new ideas of how power should function, even though they have not ultimately restructured state power" (Bishara 2017:350).

These political formations can work to delegitimize the power of the state and establish new kinds of legitimacy. They can "tacitly challenge secular or capitalist norms of state and society . . . [by] moving beyond individualistic concepts of rights [to] recognizing how politics can change on the ground in important ways, even when political structures do not budge" (Bishara 2017:353). For instance, though political state structures protect white-district domination and prevent meaningful redistribution of school funding, organizers can create regional mutual aid networks among schools, following in the long BIPOC tradition of freedom fighters. Practicing principles of mutual aid, these networks could emphasize cooperation, not competition; solidarity, not charity. Organizing from a place of abundant justice allows us to bypass the false scarcity narratives of the state and to transform politics on the ground.

★ ★ ★

In 2021, the Education Law Center honored Rochelle with a lifetime achievement award. Donning a mustard yellow linen shirt and a statement necklace, Rochelle accepted the award by reflecting on her life growing up in a working-class Black community, and the influences that shaped her:

> I grew up in South Philadelphia in a rowhouse with my father, mother, and five siblings. My dad worked at the naval base, and at night, my mom cleaned at the electric company. And during the day she cut her organizing teeth doing deep school work. She was both loved and feared by teachers, principals, and district administrators. My mom was known as that crazy woman on Reed Street with all those kids, because she not only expected, but demanded the conditions that would make the desert bear fruit. And was willing to fight for it for her children and all children. It is no surprise to me that education equity and excellence are central themes in my work.

It was clear that Rochelle inherited her mom's commitment to education organizing and an ethic of demanding "the conditions that would make the desert bear fruit." It was this spirit of determination, of making something nourishing and sweet come out of the dry and arid places, that prompted hundreds to log on to their devices and celebrate her that evening. The many well wishes that were typed into the chat window represented a veritable Who's Who of Philadelphia's education and organizing communities. These friendships had been forged over decades in the crucible of "doing deep school work"—a commitment that seemed to only grow in Rochelle's retirement. Depending on who you ask, she is either an exemplar of what one can accomplish in their retirement, or a very poor example of retired life, since she is busier now than in her paid working years.

As Rochelle saw it, her work was informed by her identity as both a teacher and an organizer. "The teacher in me deeply believes learning is transformative, and the organizer in me believes in the capacity of ordinary folk in our schools and communities to define and speak for themselves and persist, resist, and thrive." She ended her acceptance speech by interpreting a few lines from the poem, "won't you celebrate with me," by Lucille Clifton.[5]

[Clifton] begins the poem with a question: "won't you celebrate with me / what i have shaped into / a kind of life?" This line reminds me that I have been privileged to do work for all these years that perfectly aligns with my core values. That is a gift. Clifton's urging to celebrate reminds us that you can't sustain struggle without joy and celebration. I'll end with the last line of the poem, which for me expresses the ongoing struggle to achieve education equity, along with a dose of humor and drama thrown in, because in my family, we place a premium on both. Clifton ends with: "come celebrate / with me that everyday / something has tried to kill me / and has *failed*." (emphasis added)

Taking a page out of Rochelle's playbook, I end with a call to celebrate the work of racial justice warriors. Because of them, a system designed to fail Black and Brown children has failed to accomplish what it was designed to do. Let's celebrate together, that every day, freedom fighters continue to create "the conditions that would make the desert bear fruit."

# ACKNOWLEDGMENTS

It seems improbable that I would write a book about education finance and state politics—subjects that I knew very little about before this journey began. But my commitment to public education and racial justice brought me to the topic of racial inequality in school funding, and the anthropological conceit of being able to make "the strange familiar" sustained me as I trudged through stacks of spreadsheets and legislative documents. Many people supported me along the way.

I am indebted to POWER for imagining a different reality for the education funding of students of color and working toward that vision every day. Reconnecting with Rochelle Nichols-Solomon through POWER has been the biggest reward. Rochelle has a depth of experience and wisdom that is unmatched. She makes the work fun, and my friendship with her, and the rest of the Solomon family, has made our corner of Philly the best place to live. West Philly *is* the best Philly. Though she already makes an ethnographic appearance in several chapters, her influence far surpasses what appears in the index. David Mosenkis's steady and courageous moral leadership, not to mention his many important charts and graphs, put the wind in POWER's sails. He has supported my work through providing resources, reading drafts, and by thinking that this book was worth writing. Andi Moselle provides an important link between the work of the statewide campaign and the organizing efforts in Philadelphia. Her ability to attend so many meetings and keep track of everything is astounding. I am thankful to all the warriors of the statewide campaign.

My warmest thanks to the numerous people who generously lent their time to be interviewed on the issue of school funding. These included state legislators, as well as members of the PA Schools Work Campaign. In some instances, people took a professional risk in telling me about the inner workings of these places. I hope that the final analysis and product made the risk worth taking.

Former colleagues at Swarthmore College read early proposals and believed that there was a story to tell, even when I wasn't sure what that story was. My deep thanks to an incredible ensemble of faculty and staff: Edwin Mayorga, Jennifer Bradley, Lisa Smulyan, Joseph Nelson, Ann Renninger, Diane Anderson, Cathy Dunn, Ruthanne Krauss, and Elaine Allard for their support in those early inchoate stages. Elaine Allard is a colleague-friend par excellence. She was excited about this project from the get-go, gave feedback on early drafts, and seeded the idea of connecting with someone in my professional network, which turned out to be incredibly formative for the project. I miss our commutes together. Lisa Smulyan has a knack for knowing exactly what to say and when to say it in ways that have felt incredibly supportive and nurturing. I thank her for her reliability and constant willingness to read my work and provide valuable insights.

I initially thought the project was going to focus on a school funding lawsuit, but several people, including Jenna Fioravanti, Sarah Willie-LeBreton, and Elizabeth Branch Dyson didn't think it wise to hitch my wagon to a lawsuit that might take years to work its way through the courts. They were right. When that door closed, the idea of focusing on the state legislature opened, which turned out to be a fortuitous decision. I thank them for the nudge I needed to pivot.

Long before I even had an idea for this book, I knew I wanted Elizabeth Branch Dyson as my editor. That has proven to be a professional dream come true since she has stewarded many of my favorite books in education. My great thanks to Elizabeth for waving her magical editorial wand and bringing forth clarity. I am also indebted to Douglas Reed and an anonymous reviewer for their encouragement and excitement that poured from the pages. I only hope my revisions do justice to their close and conscientious reading of my work.

My colleagues at Wesleyan University provided much appreciated enthusiasm in the final push to publication. The collegiality I have with Amy Grillo, Alisha Butler, Rachel Besharat Mann, Teresa Speciale, Dana Brink, and Kim Molski made our College of Education Studies house into a home. I especially want to thank Amy and Alisha for reading over the entire manuscript and giving me terrific feedback, and Alisha for helping me make a series of changes to the final maps. Sonali Chakravarti, Camilla Zamboni, and Abigail Boggs have an innate ability to "get it" and "get it done," which has given me a sense of community and purpose at Wesleyan.

Several students provided skilled research assistance and good company along the way. I extend a warm thanks to the students at Swarthmore College, many of whom were with me since the beginning of the project: Michelle McEwen, Elizabeth Balch-Crystal, Kiara Rosario, Fouad Dakwar, Destiny Samuel, Amy-Ann Edziah, Dana Homer, and Lisa Garcia. At Wesleyan University, Ben Levin, Sofia Liaw, and Lauren Muchowski provided help during the final phases. I am honored to work with such astute, kind, and conscientious people. As well, I integrated my research into two courses that I taught and I am grateful to the students in *Educational Research for Social Change* (Spring 2020) and *Education, Race, and the Law* (Fall 2019) for being formidable intellectual interlocutors as we grappled with these issues together and sought to support the grassroots work of organizers. And I couldn't think of a better way to cap off my writing than with the students in my *Race, Nation, Empire, and Education* class (Spring 2023).

I am also thankful to the many education journalists, specifically Paul Socolar, Dale Mezzacappa, and Kevin McCorry, who provided stellar reporting on issues of school funding. I have relied on their work through the years. Connecting the thematic dots across the decades was greatly helped by their high standards in reporting. Their excellence in journalism brought color and life to the pages.

Having the time to write this book was facilitated by a National Academy of Education/Spencer postdoctoral fellowship. The fellowship also fostered meaningful relationships with senior mentors and peers including Amy Stambach, Natalie Davis, Karishma Desai, and Manuel Espinoza. I especially thank Manuel and Karishma, who have been so fully invested in me as a person and a scholar, providing sage advice and serving as emotional stalwarts.

My Penn crew runs deep, and those relationships are gifts that keep giving. Kathy Hall, Deborah Thomas, and John Jackson are each incandescently brilliant in their own way, but their kindness and generosity burn even brighter. They have been a source of warmth during some academic winters. Elaine Simon is the cool big sister everyone wished they had, and Julie McWilliams is the best grad school sister I gained, which is to say they always make me comfortable and at home. Their commitment to living in, loving, and studying Philly has deepened and strengthened my own commitment. Other friends who made my foray into academia feel like home and have journeyed the pre-tenure road with me include Shani Evans, Cecile Evers, Mariam Durrani, Gabriel Dattatreyan, Leya Mathew, and Savannah Shange. Just as Savannah influenced the shape of my dissertation, her astute insights about race and schooling have made a significant imprint on this second project. I continue to learn a great deal from her about making politics and solidarity consequential.

Longtime friends have provided social and emotional support including Michele Chen and Ed Ma, Jurica and Ray Hsu, Julie and Henry Kao, and Amy and Nafis Smith. They listened to me talk about academia and book publishing, probably well past their natural interest in the topics, and always demonstrated care and support. Cathy Candelario, my bestie since high school—though two turnpikes separate us, Cathy is always in my heart. Nothing quite compares to the kind of old friendship that allows you to pick up right where you left off. And somehow, Cyrus Candelario has fit right in, making family trips together infinitely more fun.

If it takes a village to raise a child, it takes a spectacular village to raise two children, while writing a book, and commuting across three states. That village includes the Lice crew—Angela and Jeff Curry, Hien Lu and Dylan Landis, and Vicki and Mike McGarvey—who consistently show up in big and small ways, providing good cheer, supermarket runs, dinner invitations, and cash allowances at Fiume. I am also deeply thankful to Tina Rosan, Karl Munkelwitz, and Kate Rosen for the child-sharing and second homes they provide for my children, and for their convivial company. The incredible generosity, care, and good humor of Veronica Alvarez, Baki Mani, Lei Ouyang, Asali Solomon, Linda Kim, and Lara Cohen have sustained me. Giving birth to this book was facilitated by these doulas, who provided me places to write, snacks while writing, breaks from writing, walks around the cemetery, and in many cases, their own books as inspirations of what a labor of love can produce. I also want to extend my gratitude to Amy Hillier for her GIS skills and for making my argument more compelling through visuals.

My heartfelt thanks to the family I have through marriage. Patricia and Chang Mo Liu opened their hearts and provide useful guidance, while giving us the space and freedom to make our own decisions. We are lavished with a refrigerator stocked full of Costco food and the love of extended family when we visit California. I could not ask for more. Joanne and Stephen Liu's hospitality knows no bounds. They are the most gracious hosts. Thanksgiving always features a show-stopping amount of food. They have created wonderful traditions that our children look forward to each year and regularly welcome us into the Thi fold.

To the family that raised me, Henry and Soi Chi Hugh have provided unwavering love through all these years. This has come in the form of cooking boot camp, coolers full of food from New York, delicious home-cooked meals, not-so-delicious Chinese soup concoctions, babysitting services, and even cleaning services. From them, I inherited qualities that have served me well in academia—rugged determination from my mom, and the pursuit of something you love from my dad. I am grateful that both sets of parents get along as well as they do and that we have been able to enjoy so many memorable trips together. My brother, Herbert Hugh, has provided timely words of affirmation. His simple, "You're doing great," went a long way in lifting my spirits when I was inundated. He has always been a fun and engaging uncle—getting into the rough and tumble of play during my children's younger years and giving them a well-timed "burn" that they can now appreciate in their teen and tween years. His quips and clever insights about our family dynamics often leave us in stitches.

I reserve my deepest gratitude to the family I see each day. When my children, Emily and Evie, were six and three, we were in the car and heard Asali on the radio being interviewed by Terry Gross about her first novel, *Disgruntled*. After their initial excitement passed, they turned to me and asked accusingly, "Why aren't *you* on the radio?" Though it's taken some time, I hope I have written something that is worthy of NPR. Now, as fourteen- and eleven-year-olds, they celebrate my work, encourage me, and support me, even though I have yet to land an interview with Terry Gross. They are great kids, and I'm lucky to be their mom. I hope they have witnessed me laboring for a more just world in community with others. Stan Liu, and the life we have built together, makes it all worth it. He has been profoundly there for me at every stage. That was true during my dissertating years, and even more true when I took the job at Wesleyan. I am moved when I think about all the sacrifices he has made and the labor he has put into making the "dream" of a tenure track job possible. He is talented in all the ways that matter, like ax throwing, home repair, cooking, cleaning, and surviving a zombie apocalypse. I look forward to many more years of sitting in the sunroom together, sipping our morning coffee. As my mom would say, "To Stan!"

# Timeline of Events

1983    Equalized Subsidy for Basic Education (ESBE)—provided a funding formula, but also included the first "hold harmless" language and repealed the state provision to fund 50 percent of the cost of public education.

1992    A "policy nosedive" year for Pennsylvania education funding because the state discarded the use of a formula, effectively freezing the inequities built in from ESBE's artificial limits and caps.

1998    The School District of Philadelphia faces an $85 million shortfall under the leadership of David Hornbeck.

1999    Act 46 is passed, leading to the state takeover of the School District of Philadelphia (SDP).

2000    David Hornbeck resigns as the superintendent of SDP.

2005–2014    The Pennsylvania School Funding Campaign (PSFC) years.

2008–2011    The Rendell "golden years" of school funding when there was both a formula and a funding target.

2013    News broke about earmarked funding.

2014–2016    Basic Education Funding (BEF) Commission years.

2014–2018    Campaign for Fair Education Funding (CFEF) years.

2016    The General Assembly passes Act 35, which institutes a fair funding formula, but also maintains hold harmful.

2018–    PA Schools Work campaign was formed.

2018–    POWER's 100 percent fair funding campaign was formed.

2021–    "Level Up" Equity Collaborative, a subgroup of PA Schools Work, was formed.

# APPENDIX B

### Table 2 · Members in the Campaign for Fair Education Funding

| Organizers (grassroots mobilization groups) | Policy Advocates (progressive, equity-minded, "middle" groups) | Ed Associations (unions, membership-driven organizations) |
| --- | --- | --- |
| POWER<br>• Rochelle Nichols-Solomon<br>• David Mosenkis<br>• Rev. Greg Holston<br>• Bishop Dwayne Royster<br><br>Pennsylvania Immigration and Citizenship Coalition (PICC)<br>• Sundrop Carter | Public Citizens for Children and Youth (PCCY; now "Children First")<br>• Donna Cooper<br>• Tomea Sippio-Smith<br><br>Education Law Center (ELC)<br>• Deborah Gordon Klehr<br>• Reynelle Staley<br><br>Public Interest Law Center (PILC)<br>• Michael Churchill<br><br>Pennsylvania Partnerships for Children (PPC)<br>• Joan Benso | Pennsylvania State Education Association (PSEA)<br>• Rich Askey<br>• Michael Crossey<br>• Eric Elliott<br><br>Pennsylvania School Boards Association (PSBA)<br>• John Callahan<br><br>PA Association of School Administrators (PASA)<br>• Jim Buckheit<br><br>PA Association of School Business Officials (PASBO)<br>• Jay Himes |

## Table 3 · Different Positions on School Funding in the Campaign for Fair Education Funding

| Organizers (grassroots mobilization groups) | Policy Advocates (progressive, equity-minded, "middle" groups) | Ed Associations (unions, membership-driven organizations) |
|---|---|---|
| RACIAL EQUITY 1 | RACIAL EQUITY 2 | RACIAL SCHOOL FUNDING STATUS QUO |
| Increasing state aid<br>+<br>Abolishing hold harmful | Increasing state aid<br>+<br>Accelerating funding to neediest districts (but not necessarily abolishing hold harmful) | Increasing state aid<br>+<br>Maintaining hold harmful |

# NOTES

1. Following David Mosenkis's 2016 analysis of racial bias in Pennsylvania's distribution of state education aid, I define the *racial* school funding gap as the difference between what the whitest school districts receive (relative to their fair funding formula calculation if all the money ran through the formula), and what the least white districts receive (relative to their fair funding formula calculation if all the money ran through the formula). Since the weights and methods used to construct Pennsylvania's 2016 fair funding formula were widely agreed upon, I rely on the fair funding formula to help define the racial school funding gap in state aid. In contrast, other groups define the school funding gap as the difference between how much it takes to adequately provide a basic education, and what school districts are actually allocated. The strength of this approach is that it highlights the issue of adequacy, since having a "fair share" of inadequate funding still falls short. Both approaches are valuable, but I focus on David Mosenkis's analysis to highlight that an *exclusive* focus on increasing the education budget does not address issues of racial inequity.

2. Representative Oberlander used these phrases to defend the policy of hold harmful during the first Basic Education Funding Commission hearing that took place on August 20, 2014.

3. This assumption also neglects a long history of racist housing and employment laws that curtailed Black and other nonwhite people from building wealth.

## CHAPTER TWO

1. Although the state had a funding formula in place from 2008 to 2011,

and since 2016, funding advocates express a higher regard for ESBE because of its longevity of use and because it was applied to a great proportion of the state education aid. ESBE was calculated in the following way: Factor for Education Expense (FEE) was a district's base subsidy; in 1983, this was set at $1,650. The formula for the base subsidy calculation was: district's market value/income aid ratio × the FEE × the Weighted Average Daily Membership of the district.

### CHAPTER FOUR

1. Though the state-appointed members of the newly installed School Reform Commission (SRC) oversaw the extensive growth in charter schools during its seventeen years in governance, it was the locally appointed board that ushered in the greatest charter school growth (Wolfman-Arent 2017).

### CHAPTER FIVE

1. Adding these formula weights meant that there was additional funding through changing the Average Daily Membership (ADM). ADM refers to the number of students a school district is financially responsible for. This is calculated by taking the total number of days students in the district attended and dividing it by the total number of days in a school year. Adding formula weights meant that the ADM was altered to reflect factors like poverty and number of English Learners. This "new" ADM translated into additional funding.

2. The exceptions to this demographic trend were POWER and the local chapter of the NAACP, the two Black-led organizations in the campaign, as well the ed associations that were led by white men.

3. Credited to Franklin Leonard.

4. Interestingly, in August 2020, after the spring 2020 uprisings brought on by the deaths of George Floyd, Breonna Taylor, Ahmaud Arbery, and many others, a sub-tab appeared on their website that read: "Promoting Racial Equity and Inclusion for Children of Color." Before this, there was no mention of race and inequality on their website.

### CHAPTER SIX

1. Mosenkis correctly stated that 100 percent fair funding would increase funding for the majority of state legislators by calculating the "fractional inequity" of each state legislator—that is, he calculated the percent of the school district that lies within the legislative district and then multiplied that percentage by the amount of money each district is shortchanged or overfunded. Based on that calculation, he determined that the majority of state legislators would see an increase of funding if all the money were run through the fair funding formula. However, because state legislators often have multiple school districts within their legislative district, they do not want to have to explain why they voted for a policy that would decrease state funding to one of their districts and increase it for another school district.

2. Parker represented a unique perspective on school funding. While he advocated for putting all the money through the fair funding formula, he also opposed increasing the state education budget because of his fiscally conservative stance on taxes. Moreover, one person recalled that he believed Philadelphia schools were overfunded. While I disagree with his overall position, his experience in trying to get the state legislature to drive all the money through the fair funding formula, and the obstacles he encountered along the way, is illustrative of the entrenched relationships between advocates and legislators that help to maintain the status quo. His experiences are valuable for understanding why racial inequity in school funding was such an intractable issue.

### CHAPTER SEVEN

1. ACLAMO, CASA, Education Law Center, Education Rights Network, Education Voters of Pennsylvania, Keystone Research Center, Make the Road Pennsylvania, One PA, The Public Interest Law Center, Children First (formerly PCCY), Pennsylvania Budget and Policy Center, Urban League of Philadelphia, Teach Plus, and Lutheran Advocacy Ministry in Pennsylvania. Ron Cowell, former state representative, served as an advisor.

2. For a fuller description of the methodology, see: https://leveluppa. org/wp-content/uploads/2021/04/LEVEL-UP-1-pager.pdf.

3. SDP is the largest school district in Pennsylvania, by far. As such, it would have secured a majority of the $300 million Level Up money, plus its fair funding formula share of new money.

4. Quotes here are from a text message from Rochelle Nichols-Solomon to the author on March 22, 2022.

5. "won't you celebrate with me" is from *Book of Light* (Clifton 1993):

> won't you celebrate with me
> what i have shaped into
> a kind of life? i had no model.
> born in babylon
> both nonwhite and woman
> what did i see to be except myself?
> i made it up
> here on this bridge between
> starshine and clay,
> my one hand holding tight
> my other hand; come celebrate
> with me that everyday
> something has tried to kill me
> and has failed.

# REFERENCES CITED

Agamben, Giorgio. 1998. *Homo Sacer: Sovereign Power and Bare Life*. Stanford, CA: Stanford University Press.

Ahmed, Sara. 2012. *On Being Included: Racism and Diversity in Institutional Life*. Durham, NC: Duke University Press.

Albiges, Marie. 2021. "Are Pa.'s State House and Senate Maps Gerrymandered? Depends on How You Measure Them." WHYY. https://whyy.org/articles/are-pa-s-state-house-and-senate-maps-gerrymandered-depends-on-how-you-measure-them/.

Alexander, Michelle. 2012. *The New Jim Crow*. New York: The New Press.

Atherton, Michelle J., and Meghan E. Rubado. 2014. "Hold Harmless Education Finance Policies in the U.S." Center on Regional Politics. https://williampennfoundation.org/sites/default/files/reports/Hold%20Harmless.pdf.

Augenblick, Palaich and Associates. 2007. *Costing Out the Resources Needed to Meet Pennsylvania's Public Education Goals*. Denver, CO: Augenblick, Palaich and Associates.

Austin, J. L. 1962. *How to Do Things with Words*. Oxford: Oxford University Press.

Backer, David I. 2017. "A Democrat against Democracy." *Jacobin Magazine*, May 4.

Baker, Bruce D. 2016. *Does Money Matter in Education?* 2nd ed. Washington, DC: Albert Shanker Institute.

———. 2021. *School Finance and Education Equity: Lessons from Kansas*. Cambridge, MA: Harvard Education Press.

Baker, Bruce D., Danielle Farrie, and David Sciarra. 2018. *Is School Funding Fair? A National Report Card*. 7th ed. Newark, NJ: Education Law Center and Rutgers.

Baker, Bruce D., and Preston C. Green III. 2005. "Tricks of the Trade: State Legislative Actions in School Finance Policy That Perpetuate Racial Disparities in the Post-Brown Era." *American Journal of Education* 111(3): 372–413.

Barnum, Matt. 2018. "Does Money Matter for Schools? Why One Researcher Says the Question Is 'Essentially Settled.'" *Chalkbeat*, December 17.

Behar, Ruth. 1996. *The Vulnerable Observer: Anthropology That Breaks Your Heart*. Boston, Beacon Press.

Bell, Derrick A. 1980. "*Brown v. Board of Education* and the Interest-Convergence Dilemma." *Harvard Law Review* 93(3): 518–33.

———. 2005. "The Unintended Lessons in *Brown v. Board of Education*." *NYLS Law Review* 49(4). https://digitalcommons.nyls.edu/nyls_law_review/vol49/iss4/3.

Bishara, Amahl. 2017. "Sovereignty and Popular Sovereignty for Palestinians and Beyond." *Cultural Anthropology* 32(3): 349–58.

Bissett, Janice, Arnold Hillman, and Eric Elliott. 2019. *The History of School Funding in*

*Pennsylvania 1682–2019*. Lebanon: The Pennsylvania Association of Rural and Small Schools.

brown, adrienne maree, ed. 2019. *Pleasure Activism: The Politics of Feeling Good*. Chico, CA: AK Press.

Card, David, and Alan B. Krueger. 1992. "Does School Quality Matter? Returns to Education and the Characteristics of Public Schools in the United States." *Journal of Political Economy* 100(1): 1–40.

Carter, Robert L. 1980. "A Reassessment of *Brown v. Board*." In *Shades of Brown: New Perspectives on School Desegregation*, 21–27. New York: Teachers College Press.

Clarke, Kamari. 2019. "Affective Justice: The Racialized Imaginaries of International Justice." *PoLAR: Political and Legal Anthropology Review* 42: 244–67.

Clarke, Kamari Maxine, and Deborah A. Thomas. 2006. *Globalization and Race: Transformations in the Cultural Production of Blackness*. Durham, NC: Duke University Press.

Clifton, Lucille. 1993. "won't you celebrate with me." In *Book of Light*. Port Townsend, WA: Copper Canyon Press.

Commonwealth of Pennsylvania. 2021. "Gov. Wolf Signs Budget with Largest Education Funding Increase in State History." Governor Tom Wolf, press release. https://www.governor.pa.gov/newsroom/gov-wolf-signs-budget-with-largest-education-funding-increase-in-state-history/.

Cooper, Brittney. 2018. *Eloquent Rage: A Black Feminist Discovers Her Superpower*. New York: St. Martin's Press.

Crenshaw, Kimberlé Williams, Luke Charles Harris, Daniel Martinez Hosang, and George Lipsitz, eds. 2019. *Seeing Race Again: Countering Colorblindness across the Disciplines*. Oakland: University of California Press.

Darrow, Joy. 1973. "Ghetto Housing's Future." *Chicago Daily Defender*, January 23.

*Delco Times* Editorial Board. 2019. "Editorial: The Cold, Hard Reality of Education Funding in PA." *Delco Times*, February 6: 4.

Du Bois, W. E. B. 1998. *Black Reconstruction in America, 1860–1880*. New York: Free Press.

Dudziak, Mary L. 2004. "*Brown* as a Cold War Case." *Journal of American History* 91(1): 32–42.

EdBuild. 2019. *$23 Billion*. Newark, NJ: EdBuild. https://edbuild.org/content/23-billion/full-report.pdf.

Education Law Center. 2013a. *PA Budget Analysis Funding Supplements*. Philadelphia: Education Law Center. https://www.elc-pa.org/2013/07/08/pa-education-budget-funding-for-a-few/.

———. 2013b. *Funding, Formulas, and Fairness: What Pennsylvania Can Learn from Other States' Education Funding Formulas*. Philadelphia: Education Law Center.

———. 2014. William Penn School District v. PA DOE: *Petition for Review in the Nature of an Action for Declaratory and Injunctive Relief*. Philadelphia: Education Law Center. https://edfundinglawsuit.files.wordpress.com/2014/11/williampennsd_etal_v_padepartmentofed_etal_11_10_14.pdf.

———. 2017. *Money Matters in Education Justice*. Philadelphia: Education Law Center. https://www.elc-pa.org/wp-content/uploads/2017/03/Education-Justice-Report.pdf.

Education Policy and Leadership Center. N.d. Mission Statement. https://www.eplc .org/about/mission/.

El-Mekki, Sharif. 2016. "Our School Funding System Is Racist, but Don't Call Us Racists." Philly's 7th Ward Finding Solutions for All Philadelphia Students. https:// phillys7thward.org/2016/09/our-school-funding-system-is-racist-but-dont-call-us -racists/.

Ewing, Eve L. 2018. *Ghosts in the Schoolyard.* Chicago: University of Chicago Press.

Gilmore, Ruth Wilson. 2017. "In the Shadow of the Shadow State." In *The Revolution Will Not Be Funded.* Durham, NC: Duke University Press.

Givens, Jarvis R. 2021. *Fugitive Pedagogy: Carter G. Woodson and the Art of Black Teaching.* Cambridge, MA: Harvard University Press.

Graham, Kristen A. 2018. "Days of Rain Cause Major Flooding, Ceiling Collapses at a South Philly High School." *The Philadelphia Inquirer,* September 11.

Green, Preston C., III, and Bruce D. Baker. 2021. "How Reparations Can Be Paid Through School Finance Reform." *The Conversation,* September 16. https://theconversation .com/how-reparations-can-be-paid-through-school-finance-reform-164546.

Green, Preston C., III, Bruce D. Baker, and Joseph O. Oluwole. 2021. "School Finance, Race, and Reparations." *Washington and Lee Journal of Civil Rights and Social Justice* 27(2): 483–558.

Hale, Charles R. 2006. "Activist Research v. Cultural Critique: Indigenous Land Rights and the Contradictions of Politically Engaged Anthropology." *Cultural Anthropology* 21(1): 96–120.

Hall, Kathleen D. 2002. *Lives in Translation: Sikh Youth as British Citizens.* Philadelphia: University of Pennsylvania Press.

Hanna, Maddie, and Cynthia Fernandez. 2020. "Pennsylvania Schools Need an Additional $4.6 Billion to Close Education Gaps, New Analysis Finds." *The Philadelphia Inquirer,* October 27. https://www.inquirer.com/education/school-funding -pennsylvania-lawsuit-report-20201027.html.

Hanushek, Eric A., and Alfred A. Lindseth. 2009. *Schoolhouses, Courthouses, and Statehouses: Solving the Funding-Achievement Puzzle in America's Public Schools.* Princeton, NJ: Princeton University Press.

Harris, Cheryl I. 1993. "Whiteness as Property." *Harvard Law Review* 106(8): 1707–91.

Hartman, Saidiya. 2008. *Lose Your Mother: A Journey along the Atlantic Slave Route.* New York: Farrar, Straus and Giroux.

Hawkes, Jeff. 2013. "Legislators Give $30.3M to 21 School Districts behind Closed Doors." *LNP,* Lancaster Online, July 24: 7.

———. 2018. "A Select Few Pennsylvania School Districts Get Special Deals and Millions in Bonus Funding." *LNP,* Lancaster Online, December 10.

Hess, Frederick M., and Brandon L. Wright, eds. 2020. *Getting the Most Bang for the Education Buck.* New York: Teachers College Press.

Hickernell, David. 2019. Legislation to Prohibit Special Funding for Select School Districts (Former HB 1744 of 2017–2018 Session). Pennsylvania House of Representatives. https://www.legis.state.pa.us/cfdocs/Legis/CSM/showMemoPublic.cfm ?chamber=H&SPick=20190&cosponId=28341.

Hollman, Laurie. 1992. "A Poor Neighborhood's Driving Force Mamie Nichols Makes a Big Difference in Point Breeze. Small Step by Small Step." *The Philadelphia Inquirer*, June 4: B01.

Hughes, Sarah Anne, and Angela Couloumbis. 2021. "PA's $40 Billion Budget Includes More Money for Poorest School Districts, Saves Bulk of Federal Relief Funding." *Spotlight PA (Inquirer, PennLive/The Patriot-News)*, June 25.

Jackson, C. Kirabo. 2018. *Does School Spending Matter? The New Literature on an Old Question*. Cambridge, MA: National Bureau of Economic Research. https://www.nber.org/papers/w25368.

Jackson, C. Kirabo, Rucker C. Johnson, and Claudia Persico. 2016. "The Effects of School Spending on Educational and Economic Outcomes: Evidence from School Finance Reforms." *The Quarterly Journal of Economics* 131(1): 157–218.

Jackson, C. Kirabo, and Claire Mackevicius. 2021. *The Distribution of School Spending Impacts*. Cambridge, MA: National Bureau of Economic Research. https://www.nber.org/system/files/working_papers/w28517/w28517.pdf.

Jackson, C. Kirabo, Cora Wigger, and Heyu Xiong. 2021. "Do School Spending Cuts Matter? Evidence from the Great Recession." *American Economic Journal: Economic Policy* 13(2): 304–35.

Jackson, John L. 2010. "On Ethnographic Sincerity." *Current Anthropology* 51(2): 279–89.

Johnston, Robert C. 2000. "Hornbeck Quits as Power Shifts in Philadelphia." *Education Week*, June 14. https://www.edweek.org/leadership/hornbeck-quits-as-power-shifts-in-philadelphia/2000/06.

Kelly, Matthew Gardner. 2022. "How to Reform without Reforming: School District Racial Composition and Pennsylvania's 'Fair' Funding Formula." *Education and Urban Society* 54(9): 1143–65.

Kerkstra, Patrick. 2013. "Tom Corbett Went from Establishment Republican to Tea Party Ally. Bad Move." *New Republic*, November 28. https://newrepublic.com/article/115767/tom-corbett-poll-approval-rating-pennsylvania-governor-plummets.

King, Martin Luther, Jr. 1963. "Letter from a Birmingham Jail." http://www.africa.upenn.edu/Articles_Gen/Letter_Birmingham.html.

Kingfisher, Catherine. 2007. "Discursive Constructions of Homelessness in a Small City in the Canadian Prairies: Notes on Destructuration, Individualization, and the Production of (Raced and Gendered) Unmarked Categories." *American Ethnologist* 34(1): 91–107.

Klehr, Deborah Gordon. 2019. "Pa.'s Budget Must Address Glaring Inequities in School Funding." *The Philadelphia Inquirer*, February 22. https://www.inquirer.com/opinion/commentary/tom-wolf-pennsylvania-budget-education-funding-20190222.html.

Kozol, Jonathan. 1991. *Savage Inequalities: Children in America's Schools*. New York: Harper Perennial.

Langland, Connie. 2015. "A Leadership Change at *The Notebook*." *The Philadelphia Public School Notebook* and WHYY, February 13. https://whyy.org/articles/a-leadership-change-at-the-notebook/.

Lawrence, Charles R., III. 1987. "The Id, the Ego, and Equal Protection: Reckoning with Unconscious Racism." *Stanford Law Review* 39(2): 317–88.

Leonardo, Zeus. 2004. "The Color of Supremacy: Beyond the Discourse of 'White Privilege.'" *Educational Philosophy and Theory* 36(2): 137–52.

Level Up School Funding. N.d.a. "About: School Funding in PA: We Must Do Better." https://leveluppa.org/.

———. N.d.b. "Level Up: A Proposal to Accelerate Equitable School Funding in Pennsylvania." https://leveluppa.org/wp-content/uploads/2021/04/LEVEL-UP-1-pager.pdf.

Levinson, Bradley A. U., Margaret Sutton, and Teresa Winstead. 2009. *Education Policy as a Practice of Power: Theoretical Tools, Ethnographic Methods, Democratic Options. Educational Policy.* Los Angeles: SAGE.

Liu, Roseann. 2019. "Why We Can't Afford to Leave Race Out of School Funding Conversations." Op-Ed. Color Lines WHYY, May 17. https://www.colorlines.com/articles/why-we-cant-afford-leave-race-out-school-funding-conversations-op-ed.

———. 2021. "I Said, They Said: The Ethnographic Backstage and the Politics of Producing Engaged Anthropology." *Ethnography* 00(00): 1–25.

Liu, Roseann, and Savannah Shange. 2018. "Toward Thick Solidarity: Theorizing Empathy in Social Justice Movements." *Radical History Review* (131): 189–98.

Love, Bettina L. 2019. *We Want to Do More Than Survive: Abolitionist Teaching and the Pursuit of Educational Freedom.* Boston: Beacon Press.

Marcus, George E. 1995. "Ethnography in/of the World System: The Emergence of Multi-Sited Ethnography." *Annual Review of Anthropology* 24(1): 95–117.

Massey, Douglas S. 1990. "American Apartheid: Segregation and the Making of the Underclass." *American Journal of Sociology* 96(2): 329–57.

Massumi, Brian. 1987. "Notes on the Translation and Acknowledgements." In *A Thousand Plateaus: Capitalism and Schizophrenia.* Minneapolis: University of Minnesota Press.

Mayhew, David. 2004. *Congress: The Electoral Connection.* 2nd ed. New Haven, CT: Yale University Press.

McCorry, Kevin. 2016a. "Everything You Wanted to Know about Pennsylvania's New Education Formula." *Keystone Crossroads,* WHYY, June 9: 17.

———. 2016b. "The Story of Pennsylvania's Per-Pupil School Funding in Two Maps and a Chart." *Keystone Crossroads,* WHYY, June 23: 6.

———. 2016c. "How Would Your School District Fare If Lawmakers Ramped Up the New PA Funding Formula?" WHYY/PBS/NPR, October 13. https://whyy.org/articles/how-would-your-school-district-fare-if-lawmakers-ramped-up-the-new-pa-funding-formula/.

———. 2016d. "How 25 Years of Changing Enrollment Has Created Winners and Losers in PA. School Funding." *The Philadelphia Public School Notebook,* October 24: 3.

McWilliams, Julia A. 2019. *Compete or Close: Traditional Neighborhood Schools under Pressure.* Cambridge, MA: Harvard Education Press.

Meiners, Erica R. 2007. *Right to Be Hostile: Schools, Prisons, and the Making of Public Enemies.* London: Routledge Taylor & Francis Group.

Mezzacappa, Dale. 1999. "Hornbeck Renews Criticism of PA Funding of Schools, State Policies Discriminate against Poor, Minority and Disabled Children, He Said. He Anticipated Officials' Ire." *The Philadelphia Inquirer,* November 10.

———. 2017. "A History Lesson on Historic Day for School Reform Commission." *The Philadelphia Public School Notebook*, November 16.

———. 2022. "In His Final Budget, Wolf Proposes Huge Hike in Education Spending, Including for Early Childhood." *Chalkbeat*, February 8. https://philadelphia.chalkbeat.org/2022/2/8/22924389/final-budget-gov-wolf-huge-hike-education-funding-early-childhood.

Milner, H. Richard, IV. 2012. "But What Is Urban Education?" *Urban Education* 47(3): 556–61.

Moran, Robert. 1998. "Rising Anti-Hornbeck Sentiment Led to State Takeover Legislations." *The Philadelphia Inquirer*, April 23: A19.

Morel, Domingo. 2018. *Takeover: Race, Education, and American Democracy.* New York: Oxford University Press.

Morgan, Ivy, and Ary Amerikaner. 2018. *Funding Gaps: An Analysis of School Funding Equity across the U.S. and within Each State.* Washington, DC: The Education Trust.

Morrison, Toni. 1975. "Black Studies Center Public Dialogue (Part 2)." Portland State University, May 30. https://pdxscholar.library.pdx.edu/orspeakers/90/.

Mosenkis, David. 2014. "Racial Bias in Pennsylvania's Funding of Public Schools." POWER, October. https://powerinterfaith.org/racial-bias-in-pennsylvanias-funding-of-public-schools/.

———. 2016. "Systemic Racial Bias in Latest Pennsylvania School Funding." POWER, August 25. https://powerinterfaith.org/systemic-racial-bias-in-latest-pennsylvania-school-funding/.

———. 2019. "Guest Column: Why PA Needs to Level Education Funding Field." *Delco Times*, February 16.

———. 2020. "Growing Racial Inequities in Pennsylvania School Funding." Unpublished manuscript.

Moyer, Matt, and Tom Andrews. 2018. "Browne, Schlossberg, Schweyer Secure $10 Million for Allentown School District." SenatorBrowne.com, June 22. https://www.senatorbrowne.com/2018/06/22/browne-schlossberg-schweyer-secure-10-million-for-allentown-school-district/.

Nader, Laura. 1972. "Up the Anthropologist—Perspectives Gained from Studying Up." In *Reinventing Anthropology*, ed. Dell Hymes, 284–311. New York: Pantheon Books.

National Education Association. 2020. *Ranking of the States 2019 and Estimates of School Statistics 2020.* Washington, DC: National Education Association.

———. 2022. *Ranking of the States 2021 and Estimates of School Statistics 2022.* Washington, DC: National Education Association.

Office of the Chief Clerk. N.d. *Making Law in Pennsylvania: Legislation in the PA House of Representatives. Commonwealth of Pennsylvania House of Representatives.* http://www.pacapitol.com/Resources/PDF/Making-Law-In-PA.pdf.

Ogletree, Charles J. 2004. *All Deliberate Speed: Reflections on the First Half Century of Brown v. Board of Education.* New York: W. W. Norton & Company.

Paris, Michael. 2010. *Framing Equal Opportunity: Law and the Politics of School Finance Reform.* Palo Alto, CA: Stanford University Press.

PA Schools Work. N.d. "Join a Movement That Supports Our Schools and Communities. PA Schools Work When They Are Adequately Funded." https://paschoolswork.org/.

Pennsylvania Department of Education, Data Collection Team. 2013. "Pennsylvania Public School Enrollment Reports (2012–2013)." https://www.education.pa.gov/DataAndReporting/Enrollment/Pages/PublicSchEnrReports.aspx.

———. 2021. "Pennsylvania Public School Enrollment Reports (2019–2020)." https://www.education.pa.gov/DataAndReporting/Enrollment/Pages/PublicSchEnrReports.aspx.

Pennsylvania General Assembly. 2017. "Fiscal Code—Omnibus Amendments." https://www.legis.state.pa.us/cfdocs/legis/li/uconsCheck.cfm?yr=2017&sessInd=0&act=44#:~:text=This%20act%20provides%20accountability%20for,of%20July%2011%2C%202017%20(P.L.

Pennsylvania House Appropriations Committee (D). 2018. *Hold Harmless Analysis*. Harrisburg: Pennsylvania House of Representatives. https://www.pahouse.com/Files/Documents/Appropriations/series/3056/Hold-Harmless%20Analysis%202018-19.pdf.

Pennsylvania House Democrats. 2019. "Rabb-Introduced Legislation Calls for Immediate Fair Public School Funding." *PA House News*. https://www.pahouse.com/InTheNews/NewsRelease/?id=105810.

Pennsylvania School Boards Association. 2018. "Joan L. Benso to Receive the William Howard Day Award Recognizing Outstanding Contributions to Public Education." *Advocacy & News*. https://www.psba.org/advocacy-and-news/.

Pollock, Mica. 2004. *Colormute: Race Talk Dilemmas in an American School*. Princeton, NJ: Princeton University Press.

Povinelli, Elizabeth A. 2012. "The Will to Be Otherwise/The Effort of Endurance." *South Atlantic Quarterly* 111(13): 453–75.

———. 2014. "Geontologies of the Otherwise. Theorizing the Contemporary," *Fieldsights*, January 13. https://culanth.org/fieldsights/geontologies-of-the-otherwise.

Public Citizens for Children and Youth. 2016. "Leading Education Organizations Declare Victory on Funding Formula and Call for Formula to Be Adequately Funded." Public Citizens for Children and Youth News. https://www.pccy.org/news/6078/.

———. 2021. *Hold "Harmless": A Quarter Century of Inequity at the Heart of Pennsylvania's School System*. Philadelphia: Public Citizens for Children + Youth. https://www.childrenfirstpa.org/wp-content/uploads/2021/01/PCCY-HoldHarmlessReport-2020-Final-2.pdf.

Public Interest Law Center. N.d.a. *Powell v. Ridge*. https://www.pubintlaw.org/cases-and-projects/powell-v-ridge/.

———. N.d.b. "The Campaign for Fair Education Funding. Education Equity: What We Do." https://www.pubintlaw.org/education-equity-projects/.

Rana, Junaid. 2007. "The Story of Islamophobia." *Souls* 9(2): 148–61.

Rebell, Michael A. 2009. *Court and Kids: Pursuing Education Equity through the State Court*. Chicago: University of Chicago Press.

Reed, Douglas. 2001. *On Equal Terms: The Constitutional Politics of Educational Opportunity*. Princeton, NJ: Princeton University Press.

Rhodes, Amy. 2004. "In Northeast Philly, They Are Fighting for Fair Funding." *The Philadelphia Public School Notebook.*

Rodden, Jonathan. 2019. *Why Cities Lose: The Deep Roots of the Urban-Rural Political Divide.* New York: Basic Books.

Rosa, Jonathan, and Vanessa Díaz. 2020. "Raciontologies: Rethinking Anthropological Accounts of Institutional Racism and Enactments of White Supremacy in the United States." *American Anthropologist* 122(1): 120–32.

Rothstein, Richard. 2017. *The Color of Law: A Forgotten History of How Our Government Segregated America.* New York: Liveright Publishing Corporation.

Royal, Camika. 2022. *Not Paved for Us: Black Educators and Public School Reform in Philadelphia.* Cambridge, MA: Harvard Education Press.

Ryan, James E. 1999. "The Influence of Race in School Finance Reform." *Michigan Law Review* 98(2): 432–81.

Sanchez, Claudio. 2013. "Kids Pay the Price In Fight over Fixing Philadelphia Schools." NPR, November 21. https://www.npr.org/2013/11/21/246193561/kids-pay-the-price-in-fight-over-fixing-philadelphia-schools.

Serwer, Adam. 2021. "The Capitol Riot Was an Attack on Multiracial Democracy." *Atlantic*, January 7. https://www.theatlantic.com/ideas/archive/2021/01/multiracial-democracy-55-years-old-will-it-survive/617585/.

Shange, Savannah. 2019. *Progressive Dystopia: Abolition, Anti-Blackness, and Schooling in San Francisco.* Durham, NC: Duke University Press. https://www.dukeupress.edu/progressive-dystopia.

Shaw-Amoah, Anna, and David Lapp. 2020. *Unequal Access to Educational Opportunity among Pennsylvania's High School Students.* Philadelphia: Research for Action. https://www.researchforaction.org/wp-content/uploads/2021/07/CRDC-Penn-Jan2020.pdf.

Simpson, Audra. 2014. *Mohawk Interruptus: Political Life across the Borders of Settler States.* Durham, NC: Duke University Press.

Socolar, Paul. 2013. "Increases in State Education Aid Carefully Targeted Select Districts." *The Philadelphia Public School Notebook*, July 10.

Spicka, Susan. 2019. "Letter to the Editor: Be Careful about Call for Fixing Education Funding." *Delco Times*, February 11: 1.

Tabor, Mary B. W. 1996. "Head of Philadelphia Schools Faces Battles on All Fronts." *New York Times*, July 24. https://www.nytimes.com/1996/07/24/us/head-of-philadelphia-schools-faces-battles-on-all-fronts.html.

Taylor, Keeanga-Yamahtta. 2016. *From #BlackLivesMatter to Black Liberation.* Chicago: Haymarket Books.

———. 2019. *Race for Profit: How Banks and the Real Estate Industry Undermined Black Homeownership.* Chapel Hill: University of North Carolina Press.

Thomas, Deborah A. 2009. "The Violence of Diaspora: Governmentality, Class Cultures, and Circulations." *Radical History Review* 103: 83–104.

———. 2022. "What the Caribbean Teaches Us: The Afterlives and the New Lives of Coloniality." *Journal of Latin American and Caribbean Anthropology* 27(3): 235–54.

Thompson, John B. 1990. *Ideology and Modern Culture: Critical Social Theory in the Era of Mass Communication.* Stanford, CA: Stanford University Press.

Todd-Breland, Elizabeth. 2018. *A Political Education: Black Politics and Education Reform in Chicago since the 1960s*. Chapel Hill: University of North Carolina Press.

Trouillot, Michel-Rolph. 2003. "Anthropology and the Savage Slot: The Poetics and Politics of Otherness." In *Global Transformations: Anthropology and the Modern World*. New York: Palgrave Macmillan.

Tuck, Eve. 2009. "Suspending Damage: A Letter to Communities." *Harvard Educational Review* 79(3): 409–27.

Turner, Erica O. 2020. *Suddenly Diverse: How School Districts Manage Race and Inequality*. Chicago: University of Chicago Press.

Tustin, Kevin. 2018. "Upper Darby Approves $210M School Budget with Tax Increase." *News of Delaware County*, June 23: 3.

Tyner, Adam. 2021. "How Does Money Matter for Schools?" Fordham Institute, *Flypaper*. https://fordhaminstitute.org/national/commentary/how-does-money-matter-schools.

Ushomirsky, Natasha, and David Williams. 2015. *Funding Gaps 2015: Too Many States Still Spend Less on Educating Students Who Need the Most*. Washington, DC: The Education Trust. https://edtrust.org/resource/funding-gaps-2015/.

Vaught, Sabrina Elena. 2009. "The Color of Money: School Funding and the Commodification of Black Children." *Urban Education*, September, 545–70. https://doi-org.proxy.swarthmore.edu/10.1177/0042085908318776.

Venkataramanan, Rajiv. 2010. "Rendell: Education Investments 'Moved the Ball Forward.'" *The Philadelphia Public School Notebook*, September 24. https://thenotebook.org/articles/2010/09/24/rendell-education-investments-moved-the-ball-forward/.

Vizenor, Gerald, ed. 2008. *Survivance: Narratives of Native Presence*. Lincoln: University of Nebraska Press.

Wallace, Brian. 2013. "Why the School District of Lancaster Is Financially Thriving When Similar Districts in Pennsylvania Are Failing." *LNP*, Lancaster Online, April 28.

Wasow, Omar. 2021. "'This Is Not Who We Are': Actually, the Capitol Riot Was Quintessentially American." *Washington Post*, January 7. http://www.washingtonpost.com/outlook/2021/01/07/capitol-riot-political-tradition-unamerican-history/.

Wasserstrom, Richard A. 1976. "Racism, Sexism, and Preferential Treatment: An Approach to the Topics." *UCLA Law Review* 24(4): 581–622.

Watson, Dyan. 2012. "Norming Suburban: How Teachers Talk about Race without Using Race Words." *Urban Education* 47(5): 983–1004.

Wolfman-Arent, Avi. 2017. "With SRC on the Brink, Philly Charter Schools in 'Wait-and-See' Mode." WHYY, October 31. https://whyy.org/articles/src-brink-philly-charter-schools-wait-see-mode/.

Wolfman-Arent, Avi, and Ed Mahon. 2019. "Seven Big Takeaways for Education in the New Pa. Budget." *Keystone Crossroads*, June 28. https://whyy.org/articles/seven-big-takeaways-for-education-in-the-new-pa-budget/.

Worden, Amy. 2011. "Corbett Makes Case for School Vouchers in Washington Speech." *The Philadelphia Inquirer*, May 10. https://www.inquirer.com/philly/news/local/20110510_Corbett_makes_case_for_school_vouchers_in_Washington_speech.html.

# INDEX

abundant justice, 160, 163

adequacy, 10, 118, 120, 121, 124, 147, 148, 175n1

affective justice, 112

agentive structural racism, 10, 15–16, 109. *See also* structural racism

Albert Gallatin School District, 82

Allentown (Pennsylvania), 47, 60–61

Allentown School District, 56, 59, 66–69, 97, 119; earmarked funding, 61; English Learner (EL) supplement, 60; majority-minority school population, 61

Allies for Children, 125

All Lives Matter slogan, 14

anthropology, 24–25

anti-Blackness, 76–77; anti–big city and, 77

anti-racism training, 122–25, 129

Arbery, Ahmaud, 176n4

Askey, Rich, 2, 149

Average Daily Membership (ADM), 176n1

Backer, David, 73

Badams, Jay, 65–66

Baker, Bruce, 160–61

Baker, Ella, 133

bare life education, 7

basic education funding (BEF), 2, 18, 34–39, 61, 65, 85, 95, 105–6, 125, 126, 131, 142, 150–51, 153–54

Basic Education Funding (BEF) Commission, 27, 37, 52, 65, 67–68, 90–94, 97–98, 103, 105, 108–9, 113, 125–26, 147–48, 175n2; POWER

testifying before, 99–100; school funding, 101; white rural districts, protection of, 101

Bell, Derrick, 10–11

Benso, Joan, 91, 100, 121–23

Bentham, Jeremy, 14

Biden, Joe, 70, 78

BIPOC (Black, Indigenous, people of color), 6–7, 162

Black Alliance for Educational Options, 73

Black and Brown students, 1, 3–4, 7–8, 12–13, 19, 23, 28, 30–31, 35–36, 48, 53, 61, 66, 69, 71, 78–80, 99, 118, 124, 137, 150–51, 153–54, 161, 164; as damaged goods, depiction of, 6; as shortchanged, 119; state underfunding, suffering from, 112. *See also* people of color

Blackness, 78; anti-Black attitude, 76–77

Black people, 6, 7, 11, 81; stereotyping of, 72; violence against, 121

Black Power movement, 31–32

Black youth, 79

*Book of Light* (Clifton), 178n5

Brooks, Kendra, 70

Browne, Pat, 56, 59, 67–69, 94, 99, 105, 107–8, 113

*Brown II*, 12–13, 15–16

*Brown v. Board of Education*, 10–11, 16, 25, 115; interest-convergence, 11

Buckheit, Jim, 100–102, 105

business casual Dan, 52. *See also* Dan (Democratic staffer)

California State Board of Education, 7

Callahan, John, 104, 141, 143